Get Into Veterinary School:

Insights by an Admissions Expert

For U.S. & Canadian High School, College, & Returning Adult Students

Joseph M. Piekunka, M.S.Ed.

Acknowledgements

I would like to acknowledge both the American Veterinary Medical Association (AVMA) and the Association of American Veterinary Medical Colleges (AAVMC) for allowing me to copy and reprint material from their websites. Their permission to use copyrighted material helped this book be informative and useful to pre-veterinary students. I would also like to acknowledge my loving wife, Annemarie, who suggested content enhancements and caught typos that I and my copy editor did not catch. Most importantly, she sacrificed her time to give me the many quiet hours I needed to write this book.

This book is dedicated to the memory of Priscilla Schenck, who died in late 2006. She was my administrative assistant for the ten years I directed the veterinary admissions program at Cornell University. Ms. Schenck was a valued colleague and friend. She was liked by faculty, staff and students. She had a true love and compassion for animals; she was dedicated to helping students like you understand the competitive nature of veterinary school admissions. It is hard to accept a world without Priscilla – she is truly missed by all who knew her.

Foreword

We all have a special purpose in life and my special purpose in 2006 was to write this book. I hope that by sharing my expertise in veterinary medicine admissions, readers of this book will gain a better understanding of the profession and what it takes to gain admission. It is my intention that my words will either draw you closer to the veterinary profession or perhaps change your path to a different career. Information is power and I hope my information gives you the power to make good decisions regarding the profession and admission to veterinary school.

A side note -- most pre-vets and animal lovers are concerned deeply about our environment, as is the author. To save trees, I have abandoned the convention of many blank pages in the beginning and end of the book and the starting of new chapters on a right page only.

Contents

About the Author

The author has over twenty years of experience in higher education admissions at both the undergraduate and graduate levels. He has held office with the title of director of admissions (or with higher titles) at Queens College of the City University of New York, Binghamton University of the State University of New York, Cornell University's College of Veterinary Medicine, Case Western Reserve University's School of (human) Medicine and other titles at other institutions.

Joseph Piekunka spent ten years (1995-2005) of his professional life at Cornell's College of Veterinary Medicine as Director of Admissions, where he advised thousands of students seeking admission to veterinary school. Since gaining admission to veterinary school is extremely difficult, pre-veterinary students sought his advice on how to best prepare and present their qualifications for veterinary school. Due to his wide-ranging admissions background at numerous institutions and at Cornell, he is uniquely qualified to write this book.

In addition to twenty years of admissions experience, Mr. Piekunka has vast experience in over a dozen professional organizations relating to admissions, including one important and specifically useful for this book – The Veterinary Medical College Application Service user's group. He also has experience as a graduate student advisor at Niagara University.

Mr. Piekunka now offers an advising service found at PreVetAdvising.com. This service is available to anyone who knows or is a pre-vet student, ranging from junior high-school students to older adults seeking information on how to prepare for veterinary school.

Introduction

The intent of this book is to help the reader understand how to be a competitive applicant to veterinary schools across America and Canada.

It is said that veterinary school is harder to gain admission to than medical school. Cornell's veterinary school is one of the most difficult schools to gain admission to in North America – based on GPA and test score averages and on veterinary/animal experience. The advice offered in this book is based on observations at one of the more – if not the most – difficult to enter veterinary programs in North America.

This book will give you comprehensive advice in all realms of admissions preparation: academic experience, animal and veterinary experience, extracurricular experience and personal preparation. The advice is general in nature and applies to most – if not all – veterinary schools in North America.

There are many sources of information to access during your pre-veterinary years, but some of them are not up-to-date and, therefore, not reliable. Many high-school counselors, for example, are not up-to-date on veterinary admissions requirements. Veterinarians generally do not stay up-to-date on admissions. Pre-health advisors in colleges and universities are usually the best-informed people from which to seek advice. They have very busy schedules which sometimes makes it difficult for them to stay informed on the smaller health professions. They refer to books like this book, and others such as the *Veterinary Medical School Admission Requirements* (VMSAR) to stay current.

VMSAR is a very useful resource, which has information on requirements specific for its year of publication. This book you are reading is most likely the only current publication which addresses requirements and preferred qualifications for multiple application years. It is intended to be a resource and guide throughout your pre-veterinary years.

Do you love animals, people and science equally?

Everyone would acknowledge that people thinking about a career in veterinary medicine should love animals. Some students are attracted to the profession because they want to work with animals more than people. Most animals come with a client who pays the bills; and there are people who work in the veterinary clinics and hospitals with whom veterinarians need to work. As a veterinarian, you will give bad news to your clients from time to time. You should have compassion for people. If you are choosing veterinary medicine to avoid people – think again. You should love working with people just as much as you love animals.

Likewise, your love of science will help you be a better veterinarian. Science and math are essential to the veterinary profession, and you should have an appreciation for these subjects as a pre-veterinary student. As a veterinarian, you will encounter rare diseases and cases which require you to think scientifically. If you dislike science, veterinary medicine is probably not right for you.

A love of animals alone will not heal the animals you see. However, a love of animals, people and science will make you the best veterinarian you can be.

Chapter 1:
About High School, College and Veterinary School

Veterinarians have a good amount of education before they enter veterinary school. Before going to veterinary school, you typically need four years of college (undergraduate) education. These four years will be full of math and science; if you are not fond of math and science, you may want to think very carefully whether a veterinary medicine program is right for you. After four years of undergraduate college study comes another four years of veterinary school. Not all students are inclined toward several years of college. For those who are not fond of a lot of college, perhaps a career as a veterinary technician would be more appropriate – I will discuss this later.

During your undergraduate years, you will be required by the veterinary schools to successfully complete many different college courses. To ease the transition of going to college, most students find it helpful to take similar courses at the high-school level. Here is a list of required college courses.

Required College Courses
- needed before entering veterinary school:
  English Composition
  General Biology
  General or Inorganic Chemistry
  Organic Chemistry
  Biochemistry
  Physics

All of the above core courses should be taken for a full year, except biochemistry, which can be a half-year course. In addition to the above courses, there are some courses which many of the thirty-two North American veterinary schools require as additional prerequisites.

Strongly Recommended Pre-Requisite Courses
  Genetics (20 schools require this)
  Microbiology (12)
  Statistics or Biostatistics (14, six of which require a math course)

Recommended Courses
  Animal Nutrition (2)
  Nutrition (3)
  Algebra or Trigonometry (4)
  Calculus (3)
  Anatomy and/or physiology (3)
  Animal Science (2)
  Zoology (2)
  Cellular Biology (1)
  Immunology (1)
  Vertebrate Embryology (1)

Also required are some humanities and social sciences which should automatically be met by following your course distribution guidelines of your four-year degree program. Deciding which courses to take should be mostly dependent on which veterinary schools you intend to apply to for admission. For example, the last three courses listed under 'Recommended' are each individually required at three different veterinary schools. If you are not going to apply to any of those three veterinary schools, then you may not want to crowd your undergraduate program with those courses.

Why Is Math Required?

There are many reasons. As a veterinarian, you will need to prescribe drugs for the animals you see. You must mathematically formulate the amount of the dose(s) based on the animals' weight. You also must be a good consumer of statistical information released with the latest research in your field. Math is very important.

Plan Carefully

No matter how you go about deciding which courses to take from the above lists, plan your program carefully. Veterinary school admissions offices look favorably on those applicants who are well educated. With a typical class size of 85 new students each year, the typical veterinary school will have more than 700 applicants. The veterinary schools can pick and choose who they want, and they want applicants who have strong undergraduate programs and have excellent academic achievement. Good planning of your course of study will have a significant impact on your admission to veterinary school.

If you need help planning which courses to take – and many students do – you should consider the services of your college pre-health advisor or of PreVetAdvising.com. Visit our website and make an appointment to seek advice – over the telephone – from the author of this book or his associate.

Chapter 2:
Academic Performance Versus Animal Experience

Many pre-vets who have weak academic preparation believe that veterinary schools will look favorably upon them if their animal and veterinary experience is above average. Nothing could be further from the truth. Academic preparation always trumps animal and veterinary experience.

Having ten years of pre-vet advising experience, I am aware that some of you reading about this emphasis on academic strength may be saying to yourself – "Well, he doesn't know how well I'm prepared when it comes to animal husbandry skills." It does not matter how well prepared you are when evaluating your animal husbandry skills; your academic preparation is most important. If you are successful with your academic preparation, then your animal husbandry skills will be considered.

Let me explain for those who doubt these statements why admissions offices discriminate against those with weak academic preparation. First, veterinary school is divided into two experiences. The first experience is the study of the basic medical sciences. This is typically three years of lectures and book study. There is very little, if any, hands-on experience with animals. These first three years of a veterinary education are very difficult, and some students fail out – even after being admitted with strong academic preparation in their undergraduate program. Years of high-quality animal husbandry experience will not help you during these first three years – only your academic preparation will help you here. The last part of veterinary school is working in the clinics and hospitals of the veterinary school. This usually lasts one year and your animal husbandry skills will help you in this last year of veterinary school.

Second, with so many students applying to veterinary school, why should the veterinary schools take a risk on someone with weak academic preparation? The veterinary schools do not want anyone failing out of their programs; tough academic standards during the admissions process helps reduce the number of fail-outs.

As a pre-vet advisor, the author of this book cannot overly stress this point – you must have solid academic preparation and good grades to get into veterinary school. The following chapters will help you understand how to prepare successfully for the academic hurdles your application for admission will undergo.

Chapter 3:
Academic Advice for High-School Students

Even though veterinary school is four or more years away, it is important to start planning your pre-veterinary years. There are some things that you should do in high school that will make your college experience a bit easier. As you prepare for college, do not seek the advice of only your high-school college counselor; many are unaware of the competitive nature of veterinary school admissions. In my experience, I have encountered many high-school counselors who are not even aware that applicants need to attend college before beginning veterinary school. This book and the services of PreVetAdvising.com will help you understand the many hurdles you will come across during your undergraduate/college program.

Chemistry and Calculus

First and foremost, you should take chemistry and calculus in your high-school program. During your undergraduate program, you will need to take three years of chemistry (inorganic, organic and biochemistry) to qualify for admission at most veterinary schools.   If you do not have high-school chemistry under your belt, college chemistry courses will be that much harder.   Since most college chemistry requires a good understanding of calculus (at some colleges it is required to have calculus before beginning chemistry), you should also have high-school calculus.   If you feel high-school chemistry and calculus are too difficult, perhaps you should start thinking of another profession or career track.   These courses will only become harder at the college level.   Biology and Physics are also required in college and should be taken first at the high school level.

All Colleges Are Not Equal

Learn early on in your search for a college how to discern an excellent college from a good college. In your high-school guidance office, you should find books such as: *Barron's Profiles of American Colleges* or *Peterson's Guide to Four-Year Colleges*. These books categorize each college in an admissions selectivity group.   A college that is 'Most Difficult' to gain admission to is better than a college which is 'Very Difficult.'   Many college guides published today use different language, such as 'Most Competitive' or 'Highly Selective' when they categorize the colleges.   The language is not important; it is the category or grouping of the colleges that is most important.   If you attend a college that is 'Less Competitive,' you will hurt your chances of gaining admission to veterinary school. Likewise, attending a college that is 'Most Difficult' will increase your chances of admission.

It is important for high-school students to understand that there are good colleges and better colleges.   It is also important that a pre-veterinary student not begin at a two-year college like community colleges. By their very nature, community colleges have no selectivity or competitiveness in their admissions processes. It is not impossible to gain admission to veterinary school after attending a community college; however, the probability of gaining admission decreases by attending a college with non-competitive admissions.

The theory behind the importance of admissions selectivity is tied directly to the level of teaching. All good teachers teach to the middle of the class. In a college where there is open admission, you will find very high-performing students and some low-performing students. The teachers at such a college will teach to the middle of this broad range of students. The teachers at a college such as Harvard teach to a very narrow range of high-performing students. The level of teaching is extremely high at Harvard, while the level of teaching at community colleges is much lower. Community colleges serve a very important role in our higher education system, but they are not the best colleges to prepare students for a medical education.

Now that you understand the importance of selecting an excellent college, it is important to say there are many more factors you should consider when selecting a college. For example, let us assume you have gained admission to a 'Most Competitive' college and a 'Very Competitive' college, and the 'Very Competitive' college you like substantially more than the other. You will want to attend the college which feels better to you. The happier you are in college, the better chances you have of earning good grades. Again, the admissions selectivity is only one factor to consider among many factors.

Veterinary Technology

One factor some students consider when selecting a college is studying veterinary technology at the undergraduate level. Veterinary technicians are aides, somewhat like nurses in human medicine, to the veterinarians. It is a big mistake to study veterinary technology to prepare for a medical education. Veterinary technicians learn routine procedures for nursing animals back to good health. They do not learn, as part of their program, all of the core courses and strongly recommended courses found in Chapter 1. The practical hands-on experience also is not the same hands-on experience that students learn in veterinary school. A pre-vet undergraduate program should be full of math and basic science; anything that detracts from math and basic science will likely, in the end, ruin one's chances of gaining admission to veterinary school.

Many students who do not qualify for veterinary school decide to become a veterinary technician. There is some math and science in a veterinary technology program, but far less than in veterinary school. In many cases, students with a four-year degree can attend an abbreviated two-year degree program for veterinary technology. Many courses from the four-year degree will transfer toward the two-year degree. For those who do not feel they are cut out to be a veterinary doctor, I have listed veterinary technology programs across the U.S. in appendix II. Veterinary technicians are in high demand across North America and this profession is a wonderful alternative for many students who may be thinking of a career in veterinary medicine.

Location, Location, Location

Another consideration in choosing a college is the location of your college. I am speaking of 'location' with a twist of which you may never have thought. Most students grow up in urban or suburban environments. In Chapter 8, we will discuss the importance of large-animal experience. It is most beneficial to have both small-animal and large-animal experience before applying to veterinary schools, and you may want to select a college that can give you access to large animals. A college near a racetrack or near dairy farms, or other farms with large animals might solve what some pre-vet students find to be a big problem – how to get large-animal experience before applying to veterinary schools. Again, this is just one factor among many to consider.

State or Provincial Residency

Another location issue has to do with state (when I say state I also imply province) residency. If you are from a state that does not have a veterinary school, you may want to consider establishing residency in a state with a veterinary school. Veterinary schools always give preference to students who reside in their own state. Some states allow you to establish residency during your undergraduate years. If your state does not have a veterinary school and does not have contracts with veterinary schools to give preference to your home-state residents, then you surely want to consider what state residency you will have at the time of application to veterinary schools. We will discuss residency issues in depth in Chapter 12.

Letters of Evaluation

During high school you may want to obtain some kind of formal animal experience. Formal animal experience is any experience working with animals which is formally evaluated by a veterinarian or other objective party. A letter of evaluation is needed toward the end of the experience. While veterinary schools will want to see more recent experience than your high-school years, most will also consider experience which was done during high school as long as there is a corresponding letter of evaluation.

Advanced Placement Credit

During high school, you may want to consider Advanced Placement (AP) courses. These are college level courses taught for high-school students. Some veterinary schools have very strict rules regarding their acceptance of AP credits, but generally speaking you may use AP credits to skip over introductory level courses you would otherwise need to take in your undergraduate program. For example, if you took AP Biology, you could skip introductory biology in college and enroll directly into a higher-level biology. Higher-level courses earn you more points during the admissions process. Since AP credit policies at each veterinary school can differ, and because the policies can change from time to time, the best advice I can give you is to check out the AP policies in the *Veterinary Medical School Admission Requirements*. Alternatively, you may arrange an individual counseling appointment at PreVetAdvising.com.

Choosing a College Major

Theoretically, you can study any subject so long as you have freedom to take multiple science courses. However, veterinary schools require so many different sciences and mathematics that it is difficult to prepare for multiple veterinary schools if you are not a science major. Also, if a science major with marginal grades was being compared with a music major, for example, with marginal grades, the science major would be favored. Majoring in any science is a safer bet given the varied requirements and the stiff competition for admission.

Chapter 4:
Academic Advice for College Students

The best predictor of future performance is past performance. This saying is true with professional athletes, in the financial industry and other industries, as well as in academia. Admissions committees do not want to take the risks of admitting students with a weak academic background. These committees always try to reduce their risks of admitting students who may later fail out of veterinary school by admitting only those with strong past academic performance. It is important that you understand this philosophy and that you do all you can to make your college performance the best it can possibly be.

College Course Load

Your course load is something you have control over and you would be wise not to take on too many courses at one time. This is especially true in your first term of your freshman year. Many students fumble in their coursework as they make the transition to college. Taking too many courses in your freshman year can set yourself up for failure. You should take only the number of courses you need in order to be a full-time student.

Full-time Status

Veterinary school is a full-time endeavor. The best predictor of future full-time performance is past full-time performance. Veterinary schools do not want to admit students with coursework taken on a part-time basis. Moreover, you do not want to load up on your coursework beyond what is necessary – especially in your freshman year. So take only the number of courses – usually four courses – that make you a full-time student. As you progress through each term, you will be able to predict whether you are capable of taking on a fuller schedule. If you are not capable of holding more than the minimum full-time course load, DO NOT overload yourself in future terms, even if many of your friends and classmates may be doing so. Only you can take care of yourself and your academic performance.

Grading Options

Another consideration when planning your course load is the grading options you may be able to choose. Many students are tempted to choose Pass/Fail grading options, and quite honestly the P/F option can make your courses a bit easier. To pass you usually need the equivalent of a 'D' or a 'C'. Veterinary schools do not want to see P/F grades; they want to compare your A against Johnny's 'B'. Comparing one 'P' against another 'P' gives the admissions committees no information when comparing students and selecting the class. Comparing a 'P' against a 'B' gives the student with

22

the 'B' the upper hand in the selection process. So always take courses, especially math and science courses, with the normal A B C D grading option. (In some courses, such as Physical Education, there are no options to have anything other than a P/F grade. The admissions committees are aware of this.)

Hopefully, you will never come close to having a 'D', or worse, an 'F'. However, if you feel a 'D' or an 'F' is about to descend on you, you should be aware that in most colleges you have the option of a 'W', W=Withdraw. A 'W' looks much better on a transcript than an 'F'. At some colleges, the 'W' has been replaced with a 'WP' or a 'WF'. If you feel you may end up with a 'D' or an 'F', withdraw from the course while it is still possible to record a 'WP'. Any math or science course with a 'D', an 'F', or a 'W' must be repeated or the admission committees may have strong doubt about your ability. If you repeat any course, repeat it during a full-time course load or again, the committees may doubt your true ability. Most veterinary schools set the minimum acceptable grade in science and math courses as a 'C'. In all honesty, they are hoping to see 'A's' and 'B's' on your transcript.

It is very important that you not have more than two 'W's' on your transcript. Admissions committees look at 'W's' as an indication that you might withdraw from veterinary school. Again, past performance predicts future performance. Therefore, the suggestion above (to take a 'W' instead of an 'F') comes with the caveat that you not do this more than once or twice. This also reinforces the first point in this chapter – do not overload yourself or you may have to withdraw once too often.

The Sequence of Your Courses

Another important consideration in planning a successful academic program is the timing or sequence of your coursework. As a pre-vet, you want to squeeze in every possible math and science course without overloading yourself. For this reason, it is important to begin the first term of your first year with General Biology and General/Inorganic Chemistry. All pre-vets need to take a three-year sequence of chemistry. These chemistry courses cannot be taken together, they must be taken in this sequence:

General/Inorganic Chemistry

Organic Chemistry

Biochemistry

If you begin Inorganic Chemistry in your sophomore year, you would be taking Biochemistry in your senior year. If you fail or do poorly in any one of these courses and had to repeat a course, your three-year sequence now becomes a four-year sequence and you would not finish by your senior year; you would have to extend your college timeline.

Likewise, General Biology should be taken in your freshman year as this opens the door to many other biological sciences. The later you take General Biology, the later you would begin your biology electives such as Genetics and Microbiology. Since veterinary schools' admission requirements widely differ, and since it is advisable to apply to as many different veterinary schools as possible, a pre-vet should make room in his or her program to take many different biological sciences. Starting early with General Biology is an obvious choice to make.

If I were asked to set up an ideal course schedule for pre-vet prerequisites, it would look something like this:

Freshman Year
>English Composition
>General Chemistry
>General Biology
>Statistics or Calculus (Calculus if you failed to take this in High School)

Sophomore Year
>Organic Chemistry (a difficult course)
>Physics

Junior Year
>Biochemistry
>Microbiology
>Genetics

Senior Year
>Two or three Biological Sciences (dependent on the schools to which you will apply)
>One Math course (again, dependent on your schools of application)

Another course timing issue is planning for difficult courses. If you have a particular subject that you suspect you may do poorly in, do not plan to take another subject where you suspect you may do poorly at the same time. We all have our favorite subjects and our less favorite subjects, and it is wise not to load up on less favorite subjects in the same term. One course that catches many pre-vets by surprise is Organic Chemistry. Many students do so poorly in this subject that they have to change their career path away from veterinary medicine. I recommend that you buy your organic chemistry text book a year early and study it during summer and other recesses. Be careful of your course selections during the year of Organic Chemistry.

Study Abroad

Many students desire to study abroad for one term of their college program. Study abroad experiences look good on your transcript as this indicates you want to learn about the world. However, study abroad experiences must be timed well so as not to interfere with your science prerequisites. You should never take science prerequisites abroad as an admissions committee may question whether your course in a foreign country covered the same material you would normally have in the States or Canada. It would be best to avoid studying abroad during any year in which you have a yearlong sequence of a science course, such as Organic Chemistry. Generally speaking, yearlong science courses should be completed before the junior year, so planning a study abroad experience in your junior or senior years is a safe bet. Again, do not enroll in science courses overseas.

Summer Coursework

Many students plan to do some coursework during a summer. There is nothing wrong with summer coursework as long as the course(s) you are taking are not science courses. Summer enrollment is usually part-time. Admissions committees want to see science courses completed during full-time enrollment because veterinary science courses are given during full-time enrollment. If you find you need to do some summer coursework, take social sciences or humanities courses during the summer. Also realize that summer courses are shorter and therefore more material will be taught during the week compared to fall or spring courses. Do not take a difficult subject during the summer – unless you know for certain you will have plenty of time to do your homework during the compressed summer-course timeframe.

Extracurricular Commitments

Virtually all students have a desire to get involved in extracurricular activities. This is a normal and socially healthy desire that should be encouraged. Some students get over-involved in activities that drain time and energy away from their academic performance. It is important not to get caught up in too many distractions and to leave enough time to be a good student. You have one chance to earn good grades – you will have many opportunities to get involved in activities during and after college. Chapter 10 discusses this topic more thoroughly.

Graduate Record Exam

One of the last efforts you will need to make in college for preparation for veterinary school admissions is preparing for the Graduate Record Exam (GRE). You will want to set aside a good portion of time during the end of your junior year and the first term of your senior year, and to include the summer in between these years, to prepare for the GRE. Ideally, the test would be taken in July with an opportunity to repeat it in September, if needed. The GRE is thoroughly discussed in Chapter 6.

Chapter 5:
Academic Advice for Returning Adult Students

A returning adult student is someone who is coming back to college after having been in the workforce. Many returning students are doubtful whether they have a real chance of successfully competing with students fresh out of college. The answer is that they really do have a chance and there are many returning adult students enrolled in veterinary school. (Before reading this chapter, returning students should first read Chapters 1, 2, and 4 as virtually all of the advice in those chapters applies directly to returning students.)

First Take the GRE

If the returning student has three to four years of college education, the very first thing that student would want to do is to take the Graduate Record Exam (GRE) on an unofficial basis and obtain an unofficial score. If the score is too low, then the returning student will want to think twice about whether to pursue veterinary school admissions. There are tables in the next chapter which indicate what GRE score levels are desirable with various GPA levels. It should be noted that students who repeatedly take practice GRE tests can often increase their GRE score.

After the returning student has completed a GRE self-assessment – using software and preparation books available in most bookstores – and the student is satisfied with his or her GRE scores, then it is time to begin the coursework which all students must complete. Every returning student starts from a different starting line when addressing their prerequisites. Some have a chemistry background whereas others do not. The first prerequisites a returning student should be concerned with are the chemistries – for there is a three-year sequence involved, as discussed in the previous chapter. I can give some general advice that may apply to your situation and previously completed coursework. The best advice is always individually tailored, and I strongly recommend you to seek out your pre-vet advisor or visit PreVetAdvising.com to arrange an appointment to speak with me or one of my associates.

Repeating Old Courses

Let us assume for a moment that a returning student had previously taken the chemistry sequence, yet he or she was wondering whether these courses should be taken again – so that the knowledge is current and up-to-date. If the chemistry grades were good grades, my recommendation would be to retake only biochemistry. Biochemistry is the capstone of the chemistries, and retaking only that particular chemistry should be sufficient. However, many veterinary schools have a five or ten-year limit on how old courses can be at the time of application, so if you were past their limit, my advice would be to retake whatever they require to be current. Check first with the veterinary schools of your preference about their time limits.

In the biological sciences, do not repeat coursework (except for general biology if you have a 'D'). There are plenty of new courses, like genetics and cell and molecular biology. These courses would give you new knowledge relevant to a medical education.

Again, there are so many variables a returning student can face; it is best to seek out a pre-vet advisor on campus or in the dot.com world.

Full-time Status

For the same reasons as discussed in the previous chapter, you should take your science courses on a full-time basis. You will be competing with applicants who have their coursework completed during full-time status, and they will have the upper hand when compared with others who have part-time coursework. In many cases, this means the returning student has to quit his or her job to prepare for admission. A sure way to diminish your chances of admissions is to be part-time. There are some exceptions to this rule of thumb; returning students who took full-time science course loads in the past and earned high grades may not need to do more science coursework on a full-time basis. Again, a pre-vet advisor can help you with this decision.

Degree Programs

Many returning students will ask whether a degree program is appropriate for completing the science coursework. If you already have a four-year degree, another degree is not necessary. You may take the courses as a non-matriculated (non-degree)

30

student. However, as a non-matriculated student, you may have a very difficult time getting access to courses. Most colleges have their non-matriculants register last – after many classes have full enrollment. One way of avoiding this problem is by enrolling in a pre-med post-baccalaureate program. There are websites dedicated to listing these programs, visit PreVetAdvising.com to click through to current websites on this topic.

Distance Education and CLEP

Some students ask if Distance Education – via the Internet – or CLEP tests (College Level Examination Program) may be used to satisfy pre-vet science prerequisites. The answer is usually no. Veterinary schools want to see laboratory work attached to the science coursework. Distance Education and CLEP do not provide for adequate, if any, lab work. Therefore, it is best to take science courses the old-fashioned way – on campus in a real classroom and laboratory. If a science course you wish to take does not have a laboratory requirement, you should check with your preferred veterinary schools about taking the course outside of a traditional classroom. If you want to take courses via Distance Education or CLEP, taking social sciences or humanities via these means are recommended.

Chapter 6:
Admissions Tests: the GRE and MCAT

Almost all veterinary schools require or accept the Graduate Record Exam (GRE). One veterinary school (at the University of Missouri) requires the Medical College Admissions Test (MCAT). The GRE is the test that will open the most doors to veterinary admissions and it will, therefore, receive more attention than the MCAT in this chapter.

Prepare on Your Own for the GRE

The GRE is very similar to the Scholastic Aptitude Test (SAT), which is commonly required on the East Coast at the undergraduate level. The Educational Testing Service produces both tests. To help prepare for the SAT, ETS has developed the Preliminary SAT or PSAT. Unfortunately, there is no preliminary GRE to work from. Therefore, it is the responsibility of each student to prepare for the GRE on his or her own. Most bookstores have a section of books and software that include college preparation material. Preparing on your own will often marginally increase your GRE score. Practicing the test will prepare you for the type of questions you will see on the official test. Since the GRE is now a computer-based test, you will want to eventually buy the computer-based practice software. There is also free practice software at the GRE website. Visit PreVetAdvising.com to link to the GRE website.

Many veterinary schools put equal weight on the GRE and GPA. For these schools, the lower your GPA – the higher your GRE would need to be, and vice versa. It is difficult to estimate what various combinations of GPA and GRE score levels work well, but below are estimated charts created from my twenty years of admissions experience.

There are three sections to the GRE: the Verbal Test, the Quantitative Test, and the Analytical Writing Test; the GRE percentiles below are an average of these three tests. In no way do the following numbers guarantee admission to veterinary school. These are estimates only of what GRE percentile you would want with a given GPA.

Minimum Score Levels		Optimal Score Levels	
GPA	**GRE%**	**GPA**	**GRE%**
4.0	45%	4.0	69%
3.9	50	3.9	73
3.8	55	3.8	77
3.7	60	3.7	81
3.6	65	3.6	84
3.5	70	3.5	87
3.4	75	3.4	90
3.3	80	3.3	93
3.2	85	3.2	96
3.1	90	3.1	99
3.0	95	3.0	99

Do not let these numbers scare you away from applying to veterinary school. Each veterinary school has different admission policies, and you will not know whether you are admissible unless you apply. If you score low on the GRE and you are afraid you will not gain admission because of the GRE, there are some things you might be able to do to help yourself. A common piece of advice I give to students is to practice the test – with the software that is available – three or four times to become very familiar with the test and to reduce the chances of any surprises during the official test.

If you are unhappy with the results of your own preparation for the GRE, you may want to consider a preparatory course given by a number of vendors; Kaplan and the Princeton Review to name two. These private courses can be pricey, but they can often make a difference. My best advice is to first prepare on your own before you spend good money on a preparation course.

The MCAT

The Medical College Admissions Test is accepted at five veterinary schools, four of which allow you to submit either the GRE or the MCAT scores. These four are the veterinary schools at Cornell University, Michigan State University, The Ohio State University, and Western University of Health Sciences. The fifth veterinary school, at the University of Missouri, requires the MCAT exclusively. A good score on the MCAT is a 32 out of 45 total points.

Like the GRE, there is no preliminary MCAT from which to prepare. So again, it is in your best interests to prepare on your own using the books and other preparatory materials before taking an official MCAT test. You can purchase preparation material at the MCAT website which we have linked to at PreVetAdvising.com.

Test Deadlines

Different veterinary schools have different deadlines to take the admissions test. See the chart below of VMCAS participating schools.

College of Veterinary Medicine at:	Take No Later Than*	Tests required
Auburn University	1-Jan	GRE
University of California, Davis	1-Dec	GRE
Colorado State University	3-Oct	GRE
Cornell University	15-Dec	GRE or MCAT
University of Florida	27-Oct	GRE
University of Georgia	31-Dec	GRE & GRE BIO
University of Illinois	3-Oct	GRE
Iowa State University	31-Oct	GRE
Kansas State University	3-Oct	GRE
Louisiana State University	15-Dec	GRE
Michigan State University	3-Oct	GRE or MCAT
University of Minnesota	31-Oct	GRE
Mississippi State University	1-Oct	GRE

University of Missouri	1-Feb	MCAT or GRE
North Carolina State University	3-Oct	GRE
Ohio State University	NA	GRE or MCAT
Oklahoma State University	15-Jan	GRE & GRE BIO
Oregon State University	NA	GRE
University of Pennsylvania	1-Dec	GRE
Purdue University	1-Nov	GRE
University of Tennessee	15-Jan	GRE
Virginia-Maryland Regional	1-Dec	GRE
Washington State University	3-Oct	GRE
Western University of Health Sciences	16-Oct	GRE or MCAT
University of Wisconsin	30-Nov	GRE

* 2006 data, reprinted from AAVMC.org with permission

Some students resent any form of standardized testing. It is important to remember that in order to become a licensed veterinarian, one must first pass a licensing exam, which is also a standardized test. The North American Veterinary Licensing Exam (NAVLE) is required of all students, and it is one reason veterinary schools require a standardized test for admission. Veterinary schools do not want to admit a student who does not have a good chance of passing the standardized licensing exam. Also, there will be many exams during

36

veterinary school; the veterinary schools want some reassurance that the applicants they admit are good test takers.

Chapter 7:
International Students

Canadian students are considered to be international students when applying to U.S. veterinary schools. The opposite is also true of American students. This chapter is written for international students applying to U.S. veterinary schools.

There are two big issues most international students face when applying to American educational programs: Are you proficient in the English language and can you afford an American education? When English is the first official language of the foreign country, English proficiency is usually not an issue. Students from French-speaking Quebec, however, would need to prove their English proficiency.

English Proficiency

When you go to medical school, you learn a new language of medical terms – mostly Greek and Latin terms. All medical schools, including veterinary medical schools use this language in every class. If you are not highly proficient in the English language, it will become nearly impossible to learn the unique medical language when it is taught using the English language. You must convince the admission committees that you can do well on English language tests such as the GRE Verbal and the Test of English as a Foreign Language Exam (TOEFLE). You must also convince the committees that you speak English every day and you are fluent in conversational English.

If you are not highly proficient in the English language or cannot speak conversational English with ease, then you should not consider applying to American veterinary schools. It may be beneficial to attend an American college for one year and earn grades in science courses taught in English. In fact, many veterinary schools require this of international students.

Some veterinary schools do not accept international students at all. It may be that there are serious questions raised about English proficiency and the likelihood of completion of the veterinary degree.

Enough Cash on Hand

If you are deemed fluent in the English language, then you have another big obstacle to overcome. Due to immigration issues, you must show that you have enough money in your bank to pay for four years of veterinary school tuition and room and board. In some veterinary schools, it may cost as much as $50,000 per year to attend veterinary school and live either on or off campus. At these schools, you would need to prove you have $200,000 in savings and other liquid assets to pay for veterinary school.

Many international students assume there are grants and fellowships to help pay for a medical education, but this is not the case. Grants and fellowships may be available in certain graduate programs, but they are not available in veterinary medicine. Any financial aid that may be available is almost always given only to U.S. citizens.

Therefore, if you are wealthy and you speak English very fluently, you have a chance of going to veterinary school in the U.S. One minor point which I should mention is that foreign transcripts must be sent to an international transcript evaluation company. Once your transcript(s) are evaluated and translated into English, you may then send the translations to the veterinary schools to which you may apply for admission. Below are the three most commonly used firms at which you may obtain transcript evaluations and translations.

Josef Silny & Associates, Inc.
International Education Consultants
7101 SW 102 Avenue
Miami, FL 33173
Phone: (305) 273-1616
Fax: (305) 273-1338
E-mail: info@jsilny.com
Website: http://www.jsilny.com/

World Education Services, Inc
Bowling Green Station
P.O. Box 5087
New York, NY 10274-5087
Phone: (212) 966-6311
Fax: (212) 739-6100
(800) 937-3895
E-mail: info@wes.org
Website: http://www.wes.org/

Office of International Education Services
American Association of Collegiate Registrars and
Admissions Officers
One Dupont Circle, NW, Suite 520
Washington, DC 20036-1135
Phone: (202) 293-9161
Fax: (202) 822-3940
E-mail: oies@aacrao.org
Website: http://www.aacrao.org

Test of English as a Foreign Language (TOEFL)

Test of English as a Foreign Language
TOEFL/ TSE Services
P.O. Box 6151
Princeton, NJ 08541-6151
(609) 771-7100
Website: http://www.ets.org/toefl/

Chapter 8:
The Importance of Large-Animal Experience

When veterinary students finish their four years of veterinary school, they prepare for a licensing exam – the North American Veterinary Licensing Exam (NAVLE). The NAVLE tests your knowledge on all species of animals including large farm animals. Many students want to practice veterinary medicine on small animals, also called companion animals, and they want nothing to do with large animals. The veterinary licenses issued by each state allows one to practice veterinary medicine on all species, thus the NAVLE must test your knowledge on all species.

Access to Large Animals

Most students who grow up in urban or suburban areas have a difficult time finding worthwhile experiences with large animals. This type of experience should be planned into one's college program and can be done so in a number of different ways. One option is to attend a college that has large

42

animals (most colleges with an Animal Science program have large animals) and to work or volunteer with those animals on the weekends or whenever time permits. Another option is to select a college that is in a rural area with farm animals nearby. Another option is to take one summer during your college years and live with 'Uncle Bob' and 'Aunt Bee' out in the country. Even though they might not have large animals of their own, there might be a large-animal veterinarian nearby who may be willing to take you on as a volunteer for the summer.

One cannot be shy when trying to line up some large-animal experience. Walking into a large-animal veterinary facility with a resume in hand and saying to the veterinarian: "...I am a pre-vet wanting to have some large-animal experience" is something nearly all pre-vets need to do. Veterinarians are very familiar with this type of request – chances are they made this type of request to a perfect stranger/veterinarian when they were applying to veterinary school and they know what you are up against. Some veterinarians will have a question about liability issues. If this topic comes up, be sure to quickly say that you are fully covered by health insurance in case you are injured and be willing to sign a liability/injury waiver. (The issue of general liability outside of injury to yourself is an issue that you cannot solve. If the veterinarian wants free help, he or she must be willing to take on some general liability.) When volunteering to work for free, make sure you tell the veterinarian that at the end of the experience you will want a formal evaluation for veterinary school. You may even want to hand the veterinarian the form for the letter of evaluation at the time you agree to work for free.

This may all seem like nonsense to someone who wants to work with small animals. It should be noted here that the veterinary profession was established not for small animal care. It was established centuries ago for the medical needs of farm animals. State and provincial governments fund their veterinary schools for this same reason and for the needs of public health; many diseases can cross over from animal populations to the human population. The profession is largely based in agriculture and the corresponding need for large and farm-animal medicine. Veterinary schools do not want to admit someone who has no large-animal experience when other applicants have that experience. They need to teach about all species and the NAVLE will test your knowledge on all species.

Your animal and veterinary experiences should never interfere with your academic program. Your academic preparation must come first. There will always be time to arrange animal or veterinary experience after your college program is completed; there may be very little time to repeat a course that you did poorly in due to too many time commitments outside of your academic program.

Letter of Evaluation

Whenever volunteering for a veterinary clinic, be sure you have permission and time to shadow the veterinarian. The end product of a volunteer experience is to receive a good letter of evaluation from a veterinarian – not an office manager. If you have too little time to spend with the veterinarian, the veterinarian will not be able to write genuine complimentary letter. Some clinics are so desperate for free help at all levels that they often forget pre-vets volunteer to spend time with the veterinarian. Be sure to arrange quality time shadowing the veterinarian whenever arranging any kind of animal experience.

It is important to obtain a solid number of hours working or volunteering before asking for a letter of

44

evaluation. Most letter-of-evaluation forms ask the veterinarian how much time the veterinarian worked with the candidate. If the veterinarian says he interacted with the candidate for fifty hours, that letter does not have much weight to it. I recommend that pre-vets gain about 200-300 hours of experience before asking the veterinarian to write the letter. Since you will want to have more than one letter, planning a timeline of experience - building into each experience at least 200 hours - is valuable to do early on in your pre-vet years. With thousands and thousands of competing students who have strong animal experiences, you want to fully plan and then gain valuable animal and veterinary experience.

If you have multiple opportunities to choose from, and you are not sure which to choose, contact your pre-vet advisor or access the advising services at PreVetAdvising.com.

Chapter 9:
Animal Experience and Letters of Evaluation

Obtaining animal and veterinary experience is of little use in an effort to gain admission to veterinary school if letters of evaluation are not also obtained. There are a number of variables in obtaining letters of evaluation (also referred to as letters of recommendation) of which you should be aware.

One variable is whether to ask the veterinarian to write the letter on his or her letterhead or to give him/her a letter-of-evaluation form to use. Almost every school has their own form and the Veterinary Medical College Application Service (VMCAS – pronounce vim-cas) has their own form. In fact VMCAS has two forms, an electronic form and a hard copy form. Therefore, you have many forms to choose from and it is probably best to use a neutral form – one from VMCAS. If you use a veterinary school's form, use one from your home state veterinary school or one from your favorite veterinary school. Most veterinary schools will accept a form from another veterinary school, but someone might note in the admissions committee discussions where the letter came from and maybe that the student is more interested in that school. I think it is always best to use a neutral VMCAS form.

There is no substantial difference between the VMCAS electronic and hard copy forms. Use the type with which you believe the veterinarian will be most comfortable. If in doubt, use the hard copy. Most veterinarians and others who write letters of evaluation need a constant reminder to write the letter – the hard copy sitting on one's desk is usually a better reminder than the electronic form. It is wise to kindly ask the veterinarian to inform you when the letter is completed and sent. If the veterinarian never informs you of this, then it becomes very appropriate to ask the veterinarian if he/she had time to send it. Again, many of us who write letters need gentle reminders to finish the task.

If you feel you may have a long wait before the letter is completed and sent, you may want to ask the veterinarian to give you the letter in a sealed envelope. You could then collect your letters and send them to VMCAS.

Be sure to tell the veterinarian how many hours you are listing on your application. Ask him or her if this seems accurate – he or she may get a phone call from the admissions office asking about this. The last thing you want is a major discrepancy between what you wrote in your application and what your veterinarian tells the admissions office.

The *ideal* veterinary school admissions candidate will have acquired at least three letters of evaluation and each of these letters will be based on 200-300 hours of experience. Ideally, one letter would come from a small-animal veterinarian, one from a large-animal veterinarian, one from a wildlife veterinarian, and perhaps a fourth letter from a laboratory animal setting in which the experience might be more veterinary related than animal related. Most applicants do not achieve this level of animal and veterinary experience. Those who demonstrate a broader understanding of the profession are more likely to gain admission.

Since the mechanics of asking for and receiving letters of evaluation can be rather complicated, below are the instructions posted at the VMCAS website (reprinted with permission) regarding letters of evaluation/recommendation. For very practical reasons, VMCAS promotes the electronic form over the paper form. However, you cannot access the electronic form until the year of your application.

eLOR - Electronic Letters of Recommendation

VMCAS offers an online option for completing vet school applicant evaluations called eLOR (electronic Letters of Recommendation).

By using eLOR:

Applicants can track the progress of their evaluations over the Internet -- no more worries about losing letters in the mail or wondering if their evaluators have responded.

Evaluators will find eLOR remarkably simple to use -- filling out the evaluation form is quick, straightforward, and secure. Letters of recommendation are easily incorporated into the online form.

Evaluation requirements vary by institution; please access the College Specifications page prior to sending the VMCAS evaluation form to your evaluators for specific requirements.

Here is a quick FAQ about eLOR:

What is eLOR?

eLOR stands for electronic Letters of Recommendation. It is a feature that was added to the VMCAS web application in 2003. It gives applicants and evaluators the opportunity to complete the evaluation process over the Internet. The eLOR form is an exact replica of the official VMCAS paper evaluation form. Best of all it is simple, fast, and optional.

What are the benefits of using eLOR?

eLOR benefits both applicants and their evaluators.

For Applicants: This system cuts down on the paper trail; you no longer have to mail evaluation forms to your evaluators or chase them down to find out if they have completed your evaluation. It allows you to monitor more closely the status of your evaluations by periodically logging into the system. Your minimum three evaluators can be any combination of paper or electronic form.

For Evaluators: You too no longer have to burden yourself with mailing evaluations out or the worry of having materials lost in transit. Now you only need a few minutes and a computer to complete the process! This secure service uses the same technology that our web application uses.

How does eLOR work?

Whether having the evaluations completed electronically or not, all applicants must register their evaluator's information into the eLOR section of the web application. Just designate the evaluation as 'paper' if you plan to or already have sent the official VMCAS 2007 paper evaluation form to your evaluators.

For those choosing the electronic format, enter your evaluator's information into the spaces provided. The evaluator will then receive an email requesting them to log into the secure eLOR service and complete your evaluation at their leisure. Evaluators have the option of denying your request if they, for example, wish to fill out a paper form.

Evaluators log in to the eLOR system using the information provided in the email request, fill out the required sections, and submit at a time of their choosing up to the deadline. All electronic evaluations must be completed by the application deadline. A comprehensive help section is provided and questions can be answered by a VMCAS professional by contacting us at vmcas@aavmc.org or by calling the Student and Advisor Hotline at 1 877 862 2740 (toll free).

Do I have to use eLOR?

Yes and No.

Having your evaluator complete your evaluation online instead of mailing a paper form is optional for most vet schools.

However you must at least register your evaluator into the eLOR section of the web application, even if you are planning to or have already sent out paper forms.

How do I know that the evaluation has been completed?

Log into your application (even after you have submitted) and click on eLOR. The summary screen displays the evaluator's information, including the status.

50

If the status is coded "Completed on mm/dd/yyyy" for electronic forms or filed for paper forms, then the evaluation has been successfully submitted and will be sent to the vet schools in one of the next scheduled shipments.

A status code of "Incomplete" means that the evaluator has completed any or all of the form but chose to save the evaluation as a draft instead of submitting it. Please note: If a particular evaluator's status still says incomplete as the deadline nears, then please check with your evaluator.

A status code of "Pending" means that the evaluation has not been started.

Can I submit my application before the status has changed to "Completed" or "Filed"?

Yes. As long as you have registered your minimum three evaluators in the eLOR section, you will be allowed to submit your application before the evaluations have been submitted.

How do I send out electronic committee letters?

At this time the eLOR system does not support committee or composite letters. You must still send those in as paper forms with the necessary attachments. When listing the committee/composite letter in the eLOR system, please refer to the committee chair or whoever signs the official VMCAS form. For rules on what is or is not a committee/composite letter, see the section on paper evaluations below.

Where does the evaluator place my personal letter of recommendation on the electronic form?

At the end of the electronic evaluation form, there are two free text fields provided for evaluators to cut and paste their personal letters of recommendation.

My evaluator did not receive the email request. What happened?

Assuming the email address was entered correctly, the most likely reason is that the email address that you entered for the evaluator has spam filtering which is blocking our messages. Have the evaluator disable the filter or use a different email address. If you have exhausted all options, you will have to switch to paper.

If the evaluator continues to have difficulty, please call the Student and Advisor Hotline (toll free) 1-877-862-2740 or send an email to vmcas@aavmc.org

My evaluator can't login with the username and password? What should they do now?

Have the evaluator copy and paste the username and password directly from the email into the login screen. Ensure that they are using Internet Explorer as their browser.

If the evaluator continues to have difficulty, please call the Student and Advisor Hotline (toll free) 1-877-862-2740 or send an email to vmcas@aavmc.org

Paper Evaluations

A paper VMCAS evaluation form must be attached to each personal letter of recommendation. Please notify your evaluator that the VMCAS evaluation form is mandatory for all recommendations and all questions must be answered for the following colleges: Cornell, Colorado, Florida, Kansas,

Michigan, Mississippi, Purdue, VA-MD, Wisconsin, and Prince Edward Island. Evaluation requirements vary by institution; please access the College Specifications page prior to sending the VMCAS evaluation form to your evaluators.

VMCAS will accept more than three evaluations so long as all the forms are filled out correctly. Additionally, VMCAS sends all evaluations received to all schools designated. Applicants cannot request that only certain schools receive a particular evaluation over another.

Your evaluator only needs to complete one evaluation for you; VMCAS makes the needed copies that are sent to your designated colleges.

Committee/Composite Evaluations

"Committee" evaluation letters and "composite" evaluation letters are accepted by VMCAS, as long as they are attached to a VMCAS evaluation form(s) signed by the appropriate evaluator(s) or college personnel (see explanation below).

A "committee" letter, defined by VMCAS as a single evaluation letter signed by multiple evaluators, counts as only one evaluation. A single VMCAS evaluation form should be attached to any committee letter.

A "composite" letter, defined by VMCAS as multiple letters individually signed and grouped together, can count as one to three VMCAS evaluation(s). A "composite" letter must be accompanied by the number of evaluation forms it will represent.

Chapter 10:
Activities Not Related to Veterinary Medicine

There are many activities to choose from when attending college. None of the activities you might choose should interfere with your academic program. Among the endless list of activities to choose from are: club activities, athletic activities, social activities (particularly on weekends) and student government. Then there are off-campus community service activities too numerous to list. Included in community activities are services based in religion (church choir for example). Ideally, you would want to get involved in most of these activities; realistically you do not want to overload your schedule and the number of commitments you make.

So which activities are best? The correct answer can only come from you. Engage yourself in activities that will bring you the most joy. However, if this means partying on the weekends at the expense of all else, straighten up and remember you will apply to highly competitive admission processes. A good measure of a good activity is one that will be documented through your Student Activities office or with a letter of recommendation.

Some students have unwanted documentation of public intoxication or worse, drug use. Admissions offices do not want to see this in your background. In fact, if you get involved with drugs and you acquire a felony conviction, your future is not in medicine. Most medical licenses cannot be given to a felon.

It is important at some point to undertake some leadership experience. Most veterinary schools want to see leadership experience of some kind, even if it is simply as a captain of an intramural team. Whatever your extracurricular activities are, you will probably want to briefly discuss them in your essay. You want to be able to say in your essay that you can handle a tough academic program and have a life outside of your academics.

Therefore, I have just a few pointers about extracurricular activities.

Suggestions and Advice on Extracurricular Activities
1. Be very conservative in your first term at college. Do not take on any roles it is not easy to step down from or back out of. Be a spectator who can leave an event early to do some necessary homework.
2. If you are doing well academically, slowly get involved in more activities. Live with the philosophy that academic performance is of the utmost importance. The fun activities are secondary to your college experience.
3. Athletic activities are always a healthy choice and admissions committees like to see athletic achievement.
4. If you run for a club office (treasurer, president, etc.), be extra sure you have the time. Once elected you cannot easily step

down if you start having academic problems.

5. If you run into academic problems, seek help, and if necessary, back out of any commitments you feel are stealing time away from your academic performance.
6. Pay your club dues and have your activities recorded in the Student Activities office. Admissions offices do check out the claims made on your application.
7. Have fun in college and grow to your full potential!

There are so many choices you will have in college. It is important to make good choices that will enhance you personally and enhance your application to veterinary school.

Chapter 11:
Big Mistakes You Must Avoid

There are many mistakes that applicants make from which it is hard to recover. Here is a list of the bigger mistakes you want to avoid:

1. Criminal conviction
2. Terrible grades
3. Transcript fraud
4. Lying in your application
5. Limited animal experience
6. Weak Letters of Evaluation
7. Claiming dual residency
8. Meeting only the minimum requirements
9. Unaccounted gaps of time
10. Not addressing a mistake or weakness

These mistakes can close the door to a full evaluation or from obtaining an interview. All of these mistakes are avoidable, but you must make good choices to avoid these and other mistakes. I will discuss each mistake.

1. **Criminal conviction**

A drug charge of any kind, a felony or a sexual predator conviction can each keep you out of veterinary school. In veterinary school, you will eventually have access to the pharmacy. If you have a minor drug conviction, some committees will say that you are too big a risk given all the other fine applicants. If you have a minor drug conviction, you should still apply, but be sure to address the conviction in your essay or another appropriate place. You could say it was a mistake where you learned an important lesson.

A felony is much harder to own up to and most felons cannot obtain a medical license of any kind. Veterinary schools will be very reluctant to admit someone who cannot be licensed.

A sexual predator conviction will raise a student safety question – why should a veterinary school admit someone who might harass or harm a fellow student?

2. **Terrible grades**

You could have a respectable GPA, but if you have a few 'W's', 'D's' or 'F's' among an otherwise fine transcript, questions will be raised regarding whether you could survive a rigorous program. If you apply with any of these grades, briefly explain the grade(s) in your essay or on the VMCAS explanation page. If you do not briefly explain the above grades, you would be hurting your chance of admission.

3. **Transcript fraud**

Many veterinary schools ask for transcripts in sealed envelopes collected by the applicant and submitted all together in one large envelope by the applicant.   Some applicants are tempted to steam open a transcript envelope, change a weak grade to something better, and then reseal the envelope and send it on.   These applicants do not realize that the veterinary school in which you enroll may request all new transcripts to come directly from your institution(s).   It is easy to get caught committing transcript fraud.

4. Lying in your application

It is quite safe to say that all admission committees have been lied to by at least one applicant. Since false statements and boastful claims are given to admission committees on a regular basis, admission offices are keen to verify as much information as possible. There are a number of ways admission offices check and double-check information given by applicants.   Telephone calls to student activities offices to check on the number and types of clubs and athletic teams an applicant claims membership of are routinely made.   Calls to evaluators who write letters regarding the experiences applicants claim to have are also routine. Criminal background checks are becoming more frequent and are required in some states. All applicants should be extremely careful not to exaggerate a claim for which he/she may not be given a chance to explain if the admissions office discovers it not to be fully true. An exaggeration can sometimes close the door to admission once the admissions office discovers it to be an exaggeration.

5. Limited animal experience

Limited animal and veterinary experience can make an otherwise excellent application look weak and undesirable. Do not waste your money applying early with very little experience to show to the admissions committee. Be sure you have at least one substantial experience – with 200 to 300 hours of experience – before applying. You would also want to have both large-animal and small-animal experience. Ideally, you would also have either wildlife experience or laboratory animal research experience – whichever is more appealing to you. Experiences completed after the application deadline are almost never considered.

6. Weak Letters of Evaluation

A letter of evaluation from a veterinarian who barely knows you and has an awkward time writing for you can hurt more than it helps. Applicants should have at least one letter from a veterinarian based on at least 200 hours of experience. Likewise, it is desirable to have two or three letters from veterinarians from both large-animal and small-animal experiences. Letters from wildlife or laboratory animal research experience are a real advantage, but are not necessary to gaining admission.

7. Claiming dual residency

When an applicant applies to veterinary schools through the Veterinary Medical College Application Service (VMCAS), he/she can claim residency in only one state. However, there are a small number of veterinary schools which do not participate in VMCAS. Here it is possible to claim residency in another state to which the veterinary school may give priority. It is not uncommon for one admissions director to pick up the phone to call another admissions director and ask if a particular applicant was consistent at each veterinary school with their claim of state residency. It is sometimes discovered that an applicant has claimed residency in two different states (something which is almost always impossible and often illegal). In such a case that applicant will likely be denied admission to both veterinary schools on the basis of questionable ethical behavior. Claiming dual residency is simply a dumb thing to do. We will discuss residency issues more fully in the next chapter.

8. <u>Meeting only the minimum requirements</u>

When I was Director of Admissions for Cornell's Veterinary College, I was amused by pre-vets who would say in one breath how eager they were to gain admission, and in the next breath would ask how they could minimally meet the course prerequisites. Admissions committees set minimum requirements as just that – the minimum necessary for admission. With very rich applicant pools and thousand of applicants being rejected nationwide, why would admissions committees want to accept someone who has only done the minimum? Doing just the minimum without complimenting the basics with additional coursework in the advanced biological sciences is a sure recipe for rejection.

One common mistake applicants make in this regard is not beginning basic requirements in the freshman year. Since most advanced biological sciences require basic coursework first; it is a big mistake not to begin general biology and general chemistry in the first year. (If you did not have chemistry in high school, speak with your pre-vet advisor as to whether you should take an introductory chemistry course before taking general/inorganic chemistry.)

9. Unaccounted gaps of time

Occasionally an applicant may have a summer or a year of time for which no activities or remarks are recorded in the application portfolio. This might mean that an applicant was working in a job unrelated to the profession and did not feel it was necessary to mention that job. What a big mistake!

I have seen on multiple occasions a reaction by committee members who say "...maybe this gal was in prison?" or "...maybe he did absolutely nothing for that summer?" With remarks like these and no evidence to show that he or she was indeed busy with some unrelated endeavor, the committee may quickly move on to the next applicant.

Never leave a gap of time unaccounted for in your application. Make it obvious to the readers of your application that you were always busy, even if your activities are not related to the veterinary profession.

10. Not addressing a mistake or weakness

We all have weaknesses and some of us have had failures that cannot be avoided in an application. If you have an obvious weakness or failure (an 'F' in a course, a court conviction, a college suspension for poor behavior), be sure to address the weakness or failure somewhere in your application. VMCAS offers an 'Explanation Page' which I recommend using for explaining weakness or mistakes. You want to keep your essay clean of anything that is negative. Briefly explain the weakness or failure and then move on. Do not dwell on something that is negative; state only what you feel is minimally necessary to explain the situation. Saying nothing, however, is not an option. Avoiding something that is negative and obvious will only create doubt and suspicion – which is something you do not want hanging over your application.

Chapter 12:
How State or Provincial Residency Affects Admissions

Virtually all veterinary schools receive funding from their home state or province, and as a result, virtually all veterinary schools save a majority of their seats for their home-state residents. It is always easier to gain admission in your home-state veterinary school than it is to gain admission elsewhere as an at-large applicant. Some students change their state of residency – in the end they qualify as an in-state resident in only one state and an at-large or out-of-state resident at all other veterinary schools.

There are many states and provinces which do not have a veterinary school. These states (and provinces) enter into contracts with neighboring veterinary schools. These contracts require the neighboring veterinary school to save a defined number of seats for the residents of the state without a veterinary school. A listing of contractual arrangements can be found in the *Veterinary Medical School Admission Requirements* (VMSAR). The following is a list of veterinary schools and their states or provinces.

64

United States Veterinary Medical Colleges

Auburn University (Alabama)
Colorado State University
Cornell University (New York)
Iowa State University
Kansas State University
Louisiana State University
Michigan State University
Mississippi State University
North Carolina State University
Ohio State University
Oklahoma State University
Oregon State University
Purdue University (Indiana)
Texas A & M University
Tufts University (Massachusetts)
Tuskegee University (Alabama)
University of California-Davis
University of Florida
University of Georgia
University of Illinois-Urbana
University of Minnesota
University of Missouri
University of Pennsylvania
University of Tennessee
University of Wisconsin-Madison
VA-MD Regional College of Veterinary Medicine
Washington State University
Western University of Health Sciences (California)

Canadian Veterinary Medical Colleges

Universite de Montreal (Québec)
University of Guelph (Ontario)
University of Prince Edward Island
University of Saskatchewan

There are a few states that have neither a veterinary school nor a contractual arrangement with a neighboring veterinary school. Students from these states (Connecticut, District of Columbia, Rhode Island and Vermont) are advised to move to a state with a veterinary school after checking with the veterinary school on residency qualification requirements. All applicants are advised to apply as an in-state resident or a contractual resident at one veterinary school.

Some states or provinces make it very easy to gain residency status, sometimes within six months or a year of residing in the state or province. Other states and provinces have very stringent rules on length of residency and other criteria before official residency status will be granted by the veterinary school. If you are thinking of moving to a state or province with a veterinary school in order to apply as an in-state/in-province resident, you are strongly advised to contact the veterinary school for all applicable residency qualification requirements. Do not assume that residing in a state or province will automatically give you residency status. Often it is necessary to pay income tax, change voter registration, change your driver's license and make other changes in order to be an official resident.

Voter Registration and Taxes

Some students are unsure of their residency. A common cause of confusion is a student with each parent living in a different state or province. There are a multitude of other situations which can blur the issue of residency. There are two rules of thumb that can clarify a majority of these cases most of the time. The first rule is – where is the student registered to vote? You can only vote in one state or province so voter registration is a good guideline to use. The second rule is – where does the student either pay state or provincial income tax, or where is the student claimed as a dependent on a parent's income tax form? Sometimes it is necessary to pay income taxes in two states, but you will pay *residential* income taxes in only one state or province. Taxes and voter registration provide clarity to most residency issues.

Remember, always apply to your home-state veterinary school or to a veterinary school with contractual commitments to your home-state/province.

Chapter 13:
Applying to Veterinary Schools

Applying to veterinary school is a full-time job. There are numerous forms to complete – both online and hard copy. There are deadlines to meet, essays to write, and if successful – interviews to attend. The application year, which spans from the end of your junior year (June) to May of your senior year, may be the busiest year of your undergraduate experience.

A main focus of your application experience will be understanding the Veterinary Medical College Application Service (VMCAS). This service allows you to fill out one long application form and submit to multiple veterinary schools. Almost all veterinary schools participate in VMCAS and you can check a box for each veterinary school to which you wish to apply.

VMCAS will accept your personal statement and your letters of evaluation and will forward these on to the veterinary school to which you apply. VMCAS does not handle transcripts – your transcripts must be sent from your undergraduate college(s) to the veterinary schools to which you apply. Once VMCAS has received all of your letters of evaluation, they will forward your VMCAS application to your veterinary schools. Once this occurs, you will likely receive a Supplemental Application from each veterinary school to which you applied. These will have varying deadlines and supplemental application fees. You will hear directly from the veterinary schools to which you applied regarding acceptance or rejection.

Since VMCAS will handle your letters of evaluation and not your transcripts, it is important to become and remain organized. Once you decide how many schools to which you will apply, it is recommended that you create a file folder for each school. In the front of this file folder you will want to keep a "To Do List" for that particular school. You may prefer to have one master 'To Do List' that includes all schools. Either way, most of the items on your 'To Do List' will include:

Register for the GRE
Complete the VMCAS application
Complete each Supplemental Application
Complete Transcript Request forms for each school
Complete and distribute Letter of Evaluation forms to veterinarians
Write the personal essay
Complete any state residency forms required by your school(s)
Submit the VMCAS application on-line by Oct. 1
Submit the Supplemental Applications by the posted deadlines
Pay the VMCAS and Supplemental Application fees
Respond to any correspondence from the veterinary school(s)

It is rather obvious to say that the more veterinary schools you apply to the more time and money you will spend during the application year. Therefore, when you decide how many schools to which you will apply, you must take into account the amount of time you have to complete supplemental applications and what financial limits you have for the many fees you would incur. Many applicants are surprised to find that most veterinary schools require a supplemental application and a corresponding application fee. Applying to veterinary school does not end when you submit your VMCAS application.

There is a direct link to the VMCAS website found at PreVetAdvising.com. You will want to visit the VMCAS website sometime during your junior year to learn about their latest policies and procedures.

The Best Veterinary Schools

I have often been asked which veterinary schools are the best. The answer is relatively easy to give. First, I should explain that veterinary schools are very expensive institutions to run. They generally lose money and would not be able to keep their doors open without large state subsidies. Since veterinary schools are expensive to run, I firmly believe the best veterinary schools are in heavily populated states or provinces where there is a large tax base. The larger the tax base, the easier it is to fund a veterinary school. Generous state funding is essential for a healthy and robust veterinary school. While the veterinary schools in smaller states are generally good, the best veterinary schools are in states with a large tax base and large tax revenue.

You may be asking yourself: "How does the tuition students pay affect the veterinary schools?" Tuition revenue in most veterinary schools makes up about 10% - 20% of the total revenue. Even though it

70

can be very expensive to attend veterinary school, the veterinary schools cannot rely on tuition for the majority of their revenue – they rely on their state or province for revenue. Veterinary students get an expensive education and a good deal (state subsidy) – even at the veterinary schools with the highest tuition.

Time and Money

It is important during the application year to budget both your time and money. Budgeting time during the year can be difficult considering you will likely be taking advanced biological science courses during this same time period. I recommend you take the GRE in July which would make it possible for a retake in September, if needed. It is strongly recommended that you complete and submit the VMCAS application during the summer prior to your senior year. Once you submit the VMCAS application, you will begin receiving Supplemental Applications from the veterinary schools to which you applied. Each veterinary school has a different deadline for the supplemental. You may want to record on your 'To Do List' the different deadlines for the different veterinary schools.
While only you can decide how many veterinary schools you want to apply to, it is always recommended to apply to your home-state/province veterinary school or to the veterinary schools with which your state or province has contracts. If your state has multiple contracts with many different veterinary schools, try to apply to each of the contracted veterinary schools. It would be foolish not to apply to the veterinary school(s) which favors your state or provincial residency.

Chapter 14:
Invest Time and Money

Pre-vets will spend tens of thousands of dollars to obtain a pre-vet undergraduate education, but some pre-vets are reluctant to spend another hundred dollars on books that would likely help them gain admission to veterinary school (such as GRE preparation material).

Deciding on a career in veterinary medicine is a big decision. Eight years of your life spent in college, four of these years spent in a very stressful and challenging veterinary curriculum, tens of thousands of dollars spent on both the undergraduate and veterinary degrees and a life path that would be expensive to change if you found yourself unhappy as a veterinarian. You should aid yourself as you go about making this big decision by visiting veterinary schools and buying various books that can help you prepare.

First, be sure that a career in veterinary medicine is right for you. There are many books written on the topic of careers with animals. If you visit any of the major online bookstores and type in this topic, "careers with animals," you will get a long list of books on the topic. Surely, at least one of these books would be appropriate for you. You may find a career path working with animals that does not involve veterinary medicine.

Likewise, when you start preparing for the GRE, you would find at the major online bookstores many different books and software programs to help you prepare. There is free software at the GRE website, however, that software is limited and does not allow you to prepare in a robust way. Spending $30-$40 on a book and CD-ROM for perhaps the biggest test of your life would be very wise.

If you have trouble writing essays, again there are many books to help you. Do not cut yourself short – other applicants against whom you will compete in the admissions process will be taking advantage of these resources – you should, too.

Many students are afraid of the admissions interview and there are many authors on this topic who want to help these students. Any interview can be a daunting experience, and the books available to help you will help not only with the admissions interview, but also with job interviews after veterinary school.

Every student should own a copy of the *Veterinary Medical School Admission Requirements.* This book, which is published annually by the Association of American Veterinary Medical Colleges (AAVMC), contains very useful information on each veterinary school in the U.S., Canada, and some on other continents. You will find yourself referencing this book every term when it is time to register for your college courses. You will want to have this book very handy.

It is important that every pre-vet should visit at least one veterinary school. Most veterinary schools have an annual open house, and this is a great opportunity to visit a veterinary school at which you may later spend four years of your life. When some students visit a veterinary school, they decide that veterinary school is not for them. It is much better to find this out sooner rather than later. Not everyone is cut out to go to veterinary school and visiting a veterinary school can give one a good sense of the life of a veterinary student. Some students do not like the long hours of study and the intensity of the teaching and learning that occurs at every veterinary school.

If you are admitted to veterinary school, you will be invited for a special open house (which is sometimes separate from the interview). Be sure to attend any special open house(s) when invited. You will receive a broader view of the veterinary school and will usually have time to chat directly with many veterinary students. If invited to multiple open houses, attend each and every one as the information you will obtain there will be essential in making your decision. Do not try to save a few travel dollars by skipping these opportunities for in-depth information.

Chapter 15:
The Personal Statement and Admissions Interview

The personal statement and the admissions interview are two mechanisms that allow the admissions committee to get to know the applicant. Both should be given significant preparation and attention. These two mechanisms will help distinguish you from the hundreds or thousands of other applicants.

The personal statement is something that some applicants dread. Those who do not have creative writing skills may be intimidated by the task of writing this essay. There is a six-step process which you may want to employ when undertaking this task.

1. List potential topics to discuss (see below)
2. Write an outline incorporating one or more of the topics
3. Write a rough draft of the statement
4. Put it away for a few days and review/rewrite it later
5. Show it to a few people you trust for input
6. Refine it again after receiving input

There are many topics to choose from. Here is a small list of popular topics from which many applicants select one or more topics.

1. Your motivation for becoming a veterinarian
2. Why you are well suited to be a veterinarian
3. The ideal characteristics of a veterinarian
4. Some event or experience that shaped who you are
5. What unique career path you might pursue
6. Poetry of any kind (it should say something about you or the profession)
7. The nature or direction(s) of the profession
8. An animal-related experience that influenced you
9. Any significant experience that influenced you
10. Your family & socio-economic background
11. Something challenging you overcame
12. The state of the world and the profession's role in the world
13. Something wrong about the profession and what you hope to do about it
14. Something humorous that relates to you or your application
15. Research you have done – impress them with knowledge
16. Research you hope to do and what you already know
17. Animal welfare issues and how the profession can help
18. Explain a weakness or a mistake you have overcome
19. Leadership experience that has shaped you
20. Club activities you have had and/or might undertake in veterinary school

The list goes on and on. There is no wrong topic as long as your statement is positive and lets the reader get know you. It is always a good idea to insert a little bit of humor. Faculty can get bored reading essay after essay. A small amount of humor can make the reader feel a bit more positive about you and your statement.

Sometimes we have something negative to discuss in the essay (bad grades, an indiscretion of consequence, etc.). Never dwell too long on a negative topic. Be concise and quickly conclude your point(s). Then move on to something very positive.

In most cases, there is a word limit imposed on essay type questions. Do not exceed the word limit. Again, faculty become bored reading essays; they can become grumpy if the word limit is not observed. Likewise, be sure your spelling and grammar are correct. Faculty have to score your essay and a sure way to lose points is by making them read something with poor spelling or grammar.

If you have difficulty writing your personal statement, I recommend going to your pre-vet advisor for a book or purchasing a book on how to write a good essay. Most advisors will have something on this topic and the online bookstores all have books on this topic.

The Admissions Interview

While the personal statement can be a daunting task for some, virtually everyone becomes intimidated by the admissions interview. For those who are terrified to be interviewed by faculty, you should know there are a handful of veterinary schools which do not interview at all and others that interview mostly their in-state or in-province applicants.

With good preparation, the interview does not have to be intimidating. Here is a simple list of things to prepare you for the interview.

1. Do some research on the veterinary school and formulate informed questions you could ask your interviewer when he or she gives you an opportunity.

2. Prepare your dress/suit well before the interview day.

3. If traveling a distance to the interview, give yourself plenty of time to encounter a delay of some kind. Arrive early, perhaps the night before, so that you arrive at the interview settled and with your thoughts collected.

4. Prepare yourself for some obvious questions

   a. What interests you in the profession?

   b. What motivates you to become a veterinarian?

   c. Why did you apply to our veterinary school?

   d. What do you want to do after veterinary school?

5. Prepare questions you have for the students that will give you a tour and have lunch with you.

6. Be prepared for questions on current issues and emerging diseases. Visit the avma.org site and read about 'Public Health' and 'Issues.' Formulate your opinions and thoughts about current issues.

One aspect of the interview that is important and that you have total control over is your

78

appearance. It is important to dress and to look professional. Here are some do's and don'ts.

1. Do not have any piercings other than earrings for women only.
2. Do not have wild hair dyes – your hair should look conservative.
3. Do not dress in anything less than a professional looking suit or outfit. A tie and jacket for men and a nice dress or pant suit for women. Be conservative.
4. Do cover up any tattoos as much as possible.
5. You are applying to a profession – Look Professional!

Again, your appearance is totally under your control. A conservative professional appearance will give you more confidence as you go through a long day of interviews with a variety of faculty and staff.

Be sure to have questions prepared as you will be asked: "Do you have any questions for me?" Be sure to thank your interviewer, even if you did not like the interview experience.

Your pre-vet advisor should have literature on how to prepare for an admissions interview. If not, the online bookstores have books on both the admissions interview and interviews in general. Larger brick and mortar bookstores usually have a section called 'College Guides.' There you will find all kinds of books on interviews, the essay and more.

Chapter 16:
Rejected – Should You Re-Apply?

It is very disappointing not to be admitted to veterinary school after years of hard work. Rejections are sent to at least half of the applicant pool nationwide and up to two thirds of the applicant pool when there is an upswing in applications. If you are rejected, try to look at it as a temporary bump in the road, as there is always next year.

Not everyone should re-apply though. If you do not have a significant improvement in your application the following year, it may be a waste of time, money and effort to re-apply. Many students do re-apply; in fact about one quarter of the national applicant pool each year is made up of re-applicants. If you are uncertain of re-applying, speak with your pre-vet advisor about the enhancements you will make to your application portfolio. Get a sense from your advisor if the enhancements are significant enough to re-apply. If you are no longer in school and do not have access to your pre-vet advisor, consider speaking with an advisor at <u>PreVetAdvising.com</u>.

Improve Your GRE Score

There are almost always two aspects of one's application that can be improved upon for the next year. These are your GRE test scores and the breadth of your animal and veterinary background. If you feel you did not have adequate time to prepare for the GRE test, you should put yourself through a more thorough preparation routine and then retake the GRE. Most students can marginally improve their test scores by doing this. This same advice holds true for the MCAT.

One consideration you should think about is whether you should take a private (and usually costly) test preparation course. Private test preparation courses work well for many students. Some students find no advantage in taking these courses. You will not know whether one is right for you unless you spend the money and take the course. Generally speaking, if you took a test preparation course for the SAT or ACT and the course helped you, you will probably find an advantage in taking a GRE (or MCAT) test preparation course.

One company, the Princeton Review, sometimes offers a money back guarantee if they do not improve your score. Other companies may offer this from time to time. I recommend to pre-vets to do all the self-help/self-preparation you can before spending big bucks on a course. If you do this thoroughly, it is less likely that a private course will improve your score. So if you can get a money-back guarantee on a private course, be sure to max out your self-preparation first; you might just get your money back and have a better understanding of the test!

Enhance Your Animal and Veterinary Experience

Adding to your animal and veterinary experience is a common enhancement made by students who wish to re-apply. It is often difficult to have robust experience at the time of your first application. There are four categories of experience you should try to have when applying to veterinary school. They are:

1. Small-animal experience
2. Large-animal experience
3. Wildlife or exotic animal experience
4. Research/laboratory animal experience

If you are weak in any one of these four areas on your second application attempt, try to find a volunteer experience between the time of rejection and the next application deadline. If you have this breadth of experience, you might want to consider having a significant depth of experience in one of these four categories. Breadth of experience is usually preferred over depth of experience.

Basic Science Research

Another area of enhancement you may wish to consider is gaining some basic science research if you do not already have some. This may mean working as a lab assistant on an existing project, or setting up an independent study course/research topic in which you direct yourself. The first option, lab assistant, is the most common type of research experience applicants tend to have.

If basic science research does not interest you to the point where you feel you will be miserable in the laboratory, then do not attempt it. Most veterinarians are not going to be laboratory scientists, so basic science research is not required by veterinary schools – it is only a feather in one's cap if this appears within one's application.

Additional Science Coursework

Another consideration that may apply to you is the breadth of your science coursework. If you have a minimal science background or if you have weak grades in some of your sciences, you may wish to take on some additional science coursework. I rarely recommend repeating a course unless you earned a 'D' in a required course. It is better to take higher-level sciences and do well in those than it is to repeat a course. Veterinary schools have a wide variety of requirements, so there is plenty of opportunity to take additional sciences which may open additional doors to veterinary school. Take the science courses that interest you the most. The greater your interest in a course – the better the grade you are likely to earn.

Graduate School

Some students feel the need to go onto Graduate School to enhance their veterinary school application. This is a very big and serious decision which should be reviewed with a pre-vet advisor or faculty mentor. I would never recommend Graduate School unless the graduate program was part of a "Plan B career path." To go to Graduate School simply to enhance your veterinary school application is costly and time-consuming. However, if Graduate School opens another career door through which you would want to walk if veterinary school did not pan out, then going to Graduate School would be a good plan.

If you were weak in the sciences in your undergraduate program, then taking a science program at the graduate level would be prudent. If you were strong in the sciences, then any graduate program would enhance your veterinary school application.

Offshore Veterinary Schools

One last consideration to take into account when re-applying is the option of offshore veterinary schools. Offshore schools are non-accredited schools and as such, veterinary students attending these schools have to do their clinical rotations (the last year of veterinary school) at a veterinary school with accreditation. The best students have no problem obtaining a spot in an accredited veterinary school. The weaker students may have a problem obtaining their clinical rotations; and without the rotations completed, one cannot become licensed.

Offshore veterinary schools tend to be expensive and located in impoverished areas. North American students are very wealthy in relation to the local population. If you were to consider an offshore school, you would want to visit the school and the area and inquire about the crime rates, particularly among the veterinary students. Do not ask officials for this information; ask the veterinary students who have been on the island for a year or two.

The best offshore veterinary school is the one that has been in business the longest period of time – Ross University. This school has a fine track record of placing their students in clinical rotations and there are many Ross graduates who are very successful in the U.S. It is located, however, on an impoverished island.

In my opinion, most students should not apply to offshore veterinary schools until after applying to North American schools for two admissions cycles.

84

Deciding whether to re-apply, go to Graduate School or go to an offshore school are all very difficult decisions. Find someone knowledgeable about veterinary school to discuss your ideas. If you do not have a mentor, please remember that the folks at PreVetAdvising.com are available to help you.

Chapter 17:
After Acceptance

F or those applicants who earn an acceptance to veterinary school, Congratulations! And it is not over yet! You may think that the process of enrolling in veterinary school has come to a conclusion. Yet there is important business to take care of between the months of February and May.

April 15 Decision Deadline

The first thing you need to know is that U.S. students will be given until April 15 to decide whether you will accept your offer. You may have multiple offers; you can reserve only one seat after April 15. April 15 is an important date, you must accept your offer of admission or your seat will be given to someone on the waiting list. Most applicants want to know the financial aid they will receive before April 15. In order to have a financial aid package that soon, U.S. students have to file the FAFSA (Free Application for Federal Student Aid) in late January or early February. If you fail to do this in a timely manner, you just will not have a financial aid package by April 15. An unfortunate truth at many veterinary schools is that even if you file your FAFSA early, financial aid packages are often given after April 15.

If you file your FAFSA early, some veterinary schools will have financial aid packages before your big decision has to be made – on or near to April 15. It is important not only to accept your offer of admission by April 15, you should also inform any other veterinary schools that have extended you an offer that you are not accepting their offer. As soon as you tell a veterinary school you are not accepting their offer, the admissions office will be on the phone with a wait-listed applicant giving your seat to a deserving applicant. Being on the waiting list is anxiety provoking – the sooner you give up a seat, the sooner you will reduce the anxiety of one wait-listed student.

It should be noted that no U.S. veterinary school can ask you to accept an offer of admission before April 15. If this happens, the veterinary school is breaking an agreement that all veterinary schools in the U.S. have signed. If someone somewhere is exerting pressure on you to accept before April 15, feel free to call the Association of American Veterinary Medical Colleges to report the incident. With your permission, the AAVMC will contact that person or veterinary school to remind them of the April 15 agreement. This agreement also prohibits veterinary schools from asking applicants to accept a financial aid or scholarship package before April 15.

Once you have placed your deposit and thus reserved your seat, you will be able to take a deep breath and relax – the process is almost over. All that is left to do is to arrange your housing for the fall term.

Searching for Housing

Most veterinary schools keep a housing resource list that you can access while seeking housing. Be sure to ask for housing information if it is not automatically given to you. There are usually housing websites available to help you search for housing; be sure to ask the admissions folks for this information as most of your search may be done from a distance.

Most students will rent for four years while a handful will buy property. Renters, you will likely need to sign a twelve-month lease each of the four years you are at veterinary school. College town landlords do not often give anything less than a twelve-month lease as they do not want summer vacancies.

I have always advised veterinary students to begin their housing search by May and have it concluded by July. Having an apartment by August 1 is a very comfortable feeling – you have time to set up the apartment before veterinary school begins. I strongly advise you to arrive at least one week prior to the first day of orientation to settle your apartment and to get to know the area. Once orientation and classes begin, you will not have time to settle your apartment or to cruise around town. Your time will need to be spent studying more than you desire in the first week of classes.

Personal Relationships

It is important to consider your personal life before you begin veterinary school. Veterinary school is very time-consuming and personal sacrifices are often needed in order to do well during a medical education. If you are involved in a personal relationship when admitted to veterinary school, take some time to discuss with your partner the heavy time

88

commitments you will have. Many veterinary students find themselves studying six or seven days a week with time for one night out per week. You may find this hard to believe, but after two weeks of veterinary school you will realize how intense a medical education is. Without some discussion and preparation, most partners cannot understand why the veterinary student is spending less time on the phone or with him or her after veterinary school has begun. It is difficult to convince family and friends, even pre-vets, how time-consuming a medical education is.

Many personal relationships become troubled once veterinary school begins. It is important for both the veterinary student and the partner to be prepared for life-style changes that are brought on by the intensity of a medical education. A lack of preparation can lead to academic trouble. Spending time away from studying to help a troubled relationship can put undue pressure on the student.

Communication is essential. One communication tactic may be to have your partner read these four paragraphs on personal relationships well before the beginning of veterinary school.

At some veterinary schools, the partners of veterinary students form an informal social group – something like a support group – to help both the partners and the students. The partners, however, usually have much more time to party with this social group than the veterinary students!

Chapter 18:
Do Veterinarians Need to Specialize?

The topic of specializing in the practice of veterinary medicine can be a confusing one. The veterinary degree and veterinary license allows one to practice medicine with all species of animals. However, most veterinarians focus their practice on small or large animals. This focus is not a specialization.

A specialization in veterinary medicine requires an internship and residency in one of the specialized areas of medicine. Specializations in the veterinary profession are not centered on species; they are centered on an area of medicine – surgery, radiology, reproduction, etc. Specialists have more education than the typical veterinarian, and with this extra education, specialists tend to make more money than the typical veterinarian.

You do not need to specialize; you can begin practicing veterinary medicine as soon as you have the Doctor of Veterinary Medicine (DVM) degree and have past the NAVLE (North American Veterinary Licensing Exam). If you think you may want to specialize, you do not need to decide until the last term of veterinary school. In fact, you must first pass

90

the NAVLE before you can begin a specialization. Most veterinarians do not specialize – most are general practitioners who refer rare and difficult cases to specialists.

Below is a list of the AVMA approved specialty boards, reprinted here with permission from the AVMA. Please visit their websites before calling or emailing the contacts listed. There are additional specialty organizations not formally recognized by the AVMA.

American Board of Veterinary Practitioners
Jeff Allen, Executive Director
618 Church St, Suite 220
Nashville, TN 37219
Phone: 615-254-3687
Fax: 615-254-7047
E-mail: Jallen@XMI-AMC.com
Website: http://www.abvp.com

American Board of Veterinary Toxicology
Dr. Patricia Talcott, Secretary-Treasurer
University of Idaho
Department of Food Science and Toxicology
Holm Research Center
2222 Sixth Street
Moscow, ID 83844-2201
Phone: 208-885-7081
Fax: 208-885-8937
E-mail: ptalcott@uidaho.edu
Website: http://www.abvt.org

American College of Laboratory Animal Medicine
Dr. Melvin W. Balk, Executive Director
96 Chester Street
Chester, NH 03036
Phone: 603-887-2467
Fax: 603-887-0097
E-mail: mwbaclam@gsinet.net
Website: http://www.aclam.org

American College of Poultry Veterinarians
Dr. Sherrill Davison, Secretary/Treasurer
University of Pennsylvania
382 West Street Road
Kennett Square, PA 19348
Phone: 610-444-5800, Ext 2710
Fax: 610-925-8106
E-mail: acpv@vet.upenn.edu
Website: http://www.acpv.info/

American College of Theriogenologists
Charles Franz, DVM
PO Box 3065
Montgomery, AL 36109
Phone: 334-395-4666
Fax: 334-270-3399
E-mail: charles@franzmgt.com
Website: http://www.theriogenology.org/

American College of Veterinary Anesthesiologists
Dr. John Benson, Executive Secretary
2511 CR 500E
Mahomet, IL 61853
Phone: 217-333-5345
Fax: 217-244-1475
E-mail: g-benson@uiuc.edu
Website: http://www.acva.org/

American College of Veterinary Behaviorists
Dr. Bonnie V. Beaver, Executive Director
Texas A&M University
Department of Small Animal Medicine & Surgery
4474 TAMU
College Station, TX 77843-4474
Phone: 979-845-2351
Fax: 979-845-6978
E-mail: mail@dacvb.org
Website: http://www.dacvb.org/

American College of Veterinary Clinical Pharmacology
Dr. Albert Boeckh, Secretary-Treasurer
Merial Limited
Pharmaceutical R&D
3239 Satellite Blvd., Building 500 - #258
Duluth, GA 30096

Phone: 678-638-3634
Fax: 678-638-3636
E-mail: albert.boeckh@merial.com
Website: http://www.acvcp.org

American College of Veterinary Dermatology
Ms. Alexis Borich, Executive Secretary
5610 Kearney Mesa Road, Suite B1
San Diego, CA 92111
Phone: 858-560-9393
Fax: 858-560-0206
E-mail: itchypet@aol.com
Website: http://www.acvd.org

American College of Veterinary Emergency and Critical Care
Dr. Armelle de Laforcade, Executive Secretary
Tufts Cummings School of Veterinary Medicine
200 Westboro Road
North Grafton, MA 01536
Phone: 508-839-5395 (ext. 84415)
Fax: 508-839-7922
E-mail: Armelle.delaforcade@tufts.edu
Website: www.acvecc.org

American College of Veterinary Internal Medicine
Ms. June Pooley, Executive Director
1997 Wadsworth, Suite A
Lakewood, CO 80214
Phone: 303-231-9933 or 800-245-9081
Fax: 303-231-0880
E-mail: acvim@acvim.org
Website: http://www.acvim.org

American College of Veterinary Microbiologists
Dr. Chris Hayhow, Secretary-Treasurer
30705 W. 84th Circle
DeSoto, KS 66018
Phone: 913-894-0230
Fax: 913-894-0236
E-mail: chayhow@biomunecompany.com
Website: http://www.vetmed.iastate.edu/acvm

American College of Veterinary Nutrition
Dr. Wilbur Amand, Executive Director
6 North Pennell Road
Media, PA 19063-5520
Phone: 610-892-4812
Fax: 610-892-4813
E-mail: Wbamand@aol.com
Website: www.acvn.org

American College of Veterinary Ophthalmologists
Ms. Stacee Daniel, Executive Director
PO Box 1311
Meridian, ID 83680
Phone: 208-466-7624
Fax: 208-466-7693
E-mail: office06@acvo.org
Website: http://www.acvo.org

American College of Veterinary Pathologists
Ms. Wendy Coe, Executive Director
ACVP Executive Offices
2810 Crossroads Drive, Suite 3800
Madison, WI 53718
Phone: 608-443-2466 Ext 149
Fax: 608-443-2478
E-mail: wcoe@acvp.org
Website: http://www.acvp.org/

American College of Veterinary Preventive Medicine
Dr. Russell W. Currier, DVM, MPH, Dipl. A.C.V.P.M.
Executive Vice President
P.O. Box 22219
Clive, IA 50325
Phone: 515-331-4439
Fax: 515-331-4947
E-mail: evp@acvpm.org
Website: http://www.acvpm.org

American College of Veterinary Radiology
Dr. Robert Pechman, Executive Director
777 E. Park Drive
PO Box 8820
Harrisburg, PA 17105-8820
Phone: 717-558-7865
Fax: 717-558-7841

E-mail: administration@acvr.org
Website: http://www.acvr.org

American College of Veterinary Surgeons
Alan J. Lipowitz, DVM, Executive Secretary
Ann T. Loew, EdM, Executive Director
11 N. Washington St., Suite 720
Rockville, MD 20850
Phone: 301-610-2000
Fax: 301-610-0371
E-mail: acvs@acvs.org
Website: http://www.acvs.org

American College of Zoological Medicine
Dr. Craig A. Harms, Secretary
North Carolina State University
College of Veterinary Medicine
Department of Clinical Sciences
Center for Marine Sciences and Technology
303 College Circle
Morehead City, NC 28557
Phone: 252-222-6339
Fax: 252-222-6311
E-mail: craig_harms@ncsu.edu
Website: http://www.aczm.org/aczmmain.html

American Veterinary Dental College
Colin E. Harvey, BVSC, FRCVS, DipACVS, AVDC, Secretary
University of Pennsylvania
VHUP 3113
3900 Delancey Street
Philadelphia, PA 19104-6043
Phone: 215-898-5903
Fax: 215-898-9937
E-mail: ceh@vet.upenn.edu
Website: http://www.AVDC.org

Chapter 19:
Veterinary Career Information

The American Veterinary Medicine Association maintains a website - www.avma.org - regarding veterinary career information. I encourage you to visit the AVMA website for more information on veterinary careers – particularly the statistical information they have posted there. Reprinted with permission from the AVMA, the following is a partial web page of their career information.

Today's veterinarians are in the unique position of being the only doctors trained to protect the health of both animals and people. They are not only educated to meet the health needs of every species of animal, but they play an important role in environmental protection, food safety, and public health.

Caring Professionals

According to consumer surveys, veterinarians consistently rank among the most respected professionals in the country. Currently more than 82,000 veterinarians actively practice in the United States and the profession is growing at a rate of approximately 3% per year.

In taking the Veterinarian's Oath, a new graduate solemnly swears to use his or her "scientific knowledge and skills for the benefit of society through the protection of animal health, the relief of animal suffering, the conservation of animal resources, the promotion of public health, and the advancement of medical knowledge."

Protecting the Health of Animals and Society

Employment opportunities for veterinarians are almost endless and include private or corporate clinical practice, teaching and research, regulatory medicine, public health, and military service.

Private or Corporate Clinical Practice

In the United States, approximately 67% of veterinarians are engaged in the exciting field of private or corporate clinical practice. Of these, many treat only pets such as dogs, cats, birds, small mammals (e.g., hamsters, guinea pigs), reptiles, and fish. Other veterinarians limit their practice to the care of farm/ranch animals and advise owners on the best approaches to production medicine; some exclusively treat horses; and still others treat a combination of all species.

Teaching and Research

Veterinarians may use their education to instruct veterinary students, other medical professionals, and scientists. Veterinary college/school faculty members conduct research, teach, and develop continuing education programs to help practicing veterinarians acquire new knowledge and skills.

Veterinarians employed in research at universities, colleges, governmental agencies, or in industry, are dedicated to finding new ways to prevent and treat animal and human health disorders. The public can credit veterinarians for many important contributions to human health. For example, veterinarians helped control malaria and yellow fever, solved the mystery of botulism, produced an anticoagulant used to treat some people with heart disease, identified the cause of West Nile virus infection, and defined and developed surgical techniques for humans, such as hip and knee joint replacements and limb and organ transplants.

Veterinarians who work in pharmaceutical and biomedical research firms develop, test, and supervise the production of drugs and biological products, such as antibiotics and vaccines, for human and animal use. These veterinarians usually have specialized training in fields such as pharmacology, virology, bacteriology or pathology.

Veterinarians are also employed in management, technical sales and services, and other positions in agribusinesses, pet food companies, and pharmaceutical companies. They are in demand in the agricultural chemical industry, private testing laboratories, and the feed, livestock, and poultry industries.

Regulatory Medicine

Veterinarians who work for the U.S. Department of Agriculture's Food Safety and Inspection Service (FSIS) or in a state department of agriculture protect the public from unhealthy livestock and unsafe meat and poultry. They ensure that food products are safe and wholesome through carefully monitored inspection programs.

To prevent the introduction of foreign diseases into the United States, veterinarians are employed by state and federal regulatory agencies to quarantine and inspect animals brought into the country. They supervise interstate shipments of animals, test for diseases, and manage campaigns to prevent and eradicate diseases such as tuberculosis, brucellosis, and rabies that pose threats to animal and human health.

United States Department of Agriculture (USDA) veterinarians in the Animal and Plant Health Inspection Service (APHIS) monitor the development and testing of new vaccines to ensure their safety and effectiveness. APHIS veterinarians are also responsible for enforcing humane laws for the treatment of animals. Other branches of the USDA such as the Agricultural Research Service (ARS) and the Cooperative State Research, Education, and Extension Service (CSREES), also have employment opportunities for veterinarians.

Public Health

Veterinarians serve as epidemiologists in city, county, state, and federal agencies investigating animal and human disease outbreaks such as food-borne illnesses, influenza, rabies, Lyme disease, and West Nile viral encephalitis. They also help ensure the safety of food processing plants, restaurants, and water supplies.

Veterinarians working in environmental health programs study the effects of pesticides, industrial pollutants, and other contaminants on animals and people. At the U.S. Food and Drug Administration (FDA), veterinarians evaluate the safety and efficacy of medicines and food additives. Veterinarians also work at the Agricultural Research Service, Fish and Wildlife Service, Environmental Protection Agency, Centers for Disease Control and Prevention, National Library of Medicine, and National Institutes of Health. Many of these veterinarians serve in the U.S. Public Health

Service Commissioned Corps.

Veterinarians also help to protect the health and safety of animals and people in the Department of Homeland Security through their work in developing antiterrorism procedures and protocols.

Military Service

Veterinarians in the U.S. Army Veterinary Corps are at the forefront in protecting the United States against bioterrorism. They are responsible for food safety, veterinary care of government-owned animals, and biomedical research and development. Officers with special training in laboratory animal medicine, pathology, microbiology, or related disciplines, conduct research in military and other governmental agencies.

In the U.S. Air Force, veterinarians serve in the Biomedical Science Corps as public health officers. They manage communicable disease control programs at air force bases around the world and work towards halting the spread of HIV, influenza, hepatitis, and other infectious diseases through education, surveillance, and vaccination.

Other Professional Activities

Zoologic medicine, aquatic animal medicine, aerospace medicine (shuttle astronauts), animal shelter medicine, sports medicine (race horses,

100

greyhounds), animal-assisted activity and therapy programs, and wildlife management also employ veterinarians.

Is Veterinary Medicine Right for You?

Today's veterinarians are extremely dedicated and willing to work long, difficult hours to save the life of an animal or help solve a public health crisis. Among the personal attributes that contribute to a successful career in veterinary medicine are:

A scientific mind — Individuals who are interested in veterinary medicine should have an inquiring mind and keen powers of observation. Aptitude and interest in the biological sciences are important. Veterinarians must maintain a lifelong interest in scientific learning, and must genuinely like and understand animals.

Good communication skills — Veterinarians should be able to meet, talk, and work well with a variety of people. Compassion is an essential attribute for success, especially for veterinarians working with pet owners who form strong bonds with their pets.

Management experience — Many work environments (e.g., private or corporate clinical practice, governmental agencies, public health programs) require that veterinarians manage other employees. Basic managerial and leadership skills training make these positions much more rewarding.

A Bright Future

Employment opportunities for veterinarians are expected to keep pace with those of other professions. Positions exist for which postgraduate education in molecular biology, laboratory animal medicine, toxicology, immunology, diagnostic pathology, environmental medicine, or other

101

specialties is preferred or required. The benefit of using scientific methods to breed and raise livestock, poultry, and fish, together with a growing need for effective public health and disease control programs, will continue to demand the expertise of veterinarians.

For More Information

The AVMA has produced a video and a CD-ROM, Veterinary Medicine — Dedicated to Service, which profiles veterinarians engaged in a variety of professional activities in different parts of the United States. For more information, call the AVMA Communications Division at 847-925-8070, ext. 6617.

Appendix I:
Veterinary Schools and Organizations

Alabama

Auburn University
College of Veterinary Medicine
104 Greene Hall
Auburn University, AL 36849
Telephone: 334-844-4546
www.vetmed.auburn.edu

Tuskegee University
School of Veterinary Medicine
Tuskegee, AL 36088
Telephone: 334-727-8174
www.tuskegee.edu

California

University of California
School of Veterinary Medicine
Davis, CA 95616-8734
Telephone: 530-752-1360
www.vetmed.ucdavis.edu

Western University of Health Sciences
College of Veterinary Medicine
309 E Second Street - College Plaza
Pomona, CA, 91766-1854
Telephone: 909-469-5628
www.westernu.edu/cvm.html

Colorado

Colorado State University
College of Veterinary Medicine
and Biomedical Sciences
Fort Collins, CO 80523
Telephone: 970-491-7051
www.cvmbs.colostate.edu

Florida

University of Florida
College of Veterinary Medicine
PO Box 100125
Gainesville, FL 32610
Telephone: 352-392-4700
www.vetmed.ufl.edu

Georgia

University of Georgia
College of Veterinary Medicine
Athens, GA 30602
Telephone: 706-542-3461
www.vet.uga.edu

Illinois

University of Illinois
College of Veterinary Medicine
2001 South Lincoln Avenue
Urbana, IL 61802
Telephone: 217-333-2760
www.cvm.uiuc.edu

Indiana

Purdue University
School of Veterinary Medicine
1240 Lynn Hall
West Lafayette, IN 47907
Telephone: 765-494-7607
www.vet.purdue.edu

Iowa

Iowa State University
College of Veterinary Medicine
Ames, IA 50011
Telephone: 515-294-1242
www.vetmed.iastate.edu

Kansas

Kansas State University
College of Veterinary Medicine
Manhattan, KS 66506
Telephone: 785-532-5660
www.vet.ksu.edu

Louisiana

Louisiana State University
School of Veterinary Medicine
Baton Rouge, LA 70803-8402
Telephone: 225-578-9900
www.vetmed.lsu.edu

Massachusetts

Tufts University
School of Veterinary Medicine
200 Westboro Road
North Grafton, MA 01536
Telephone: 508-839-5302
www.tufts.edu/vet

Michigan

Michigan State University
College of Veterinary Medicine
G-100 Veterinary Medical Center
East Lansing, MI 48824
Telephone: 517-355-6509
www.cvm.msu.edu

Minnesota

The University of Minnesota
College of Veterinary Medicine
1365 Gortner Avenue
St. Paul, MN 55108
Telephone: 612-624-9227
www.cvm.umn.edu

Mississippi

Mississippi State University
College of Veterinary Medicine
Mississippi State, MS 39762
Telephone: 662-325-3432
www.cvm.msstate.edu

Missouri

University of Missouri-Columbia
College of Veterinary Medicine
Columbia, MO 65211
Telephone: 573-882-3877
www.cvm.missouri.edu

New York

Cornell University
College of Veterinary Medicine
Ithaca, NY 14853
Telephone: 607-253-3700
www.vet.cornell.edu

North Carolina

North Carolina State University
College of Veterinary Medicine
4700 Hillsborough Street
Raleigh, NC 27606
Telephone: 919-513-6210
www.cvm.ncsu.edu

Ohio

The Ohio State University
College of Veterinary Medicine
1900 Coffey Road
Columbus, OH 43210
Telephone: 614-292-1171
www.vet.ohio-state.edu

Oklahoma

Oklahoma State University
College of Veterinary Medicine
Stillwater, OK 74078
Telephone: 405-744-6595
www.cvm.okstate.edu

Oregon

Oregon State University
College of Veterinary Medicine
Corvallis, OR 97331
Telephone: 541-737-2098
www.vet.orst.edu

Pennsylvania

University of Pennsylvania
School of Veterinary Medicine
3800 Spruce Street
Philadelphia, PA 19104
Telephone: 215-898-5438
www.vet.upenn.edu

Tennessee

University of Tennessee
College of Veterinary Medicine
2407 River Drive
Knoxville, TN 37996
Telephone: 865-974-7262
www.vet.utk.edu

Texas

Texas A&M University
College of Veterinary Medicine & Biomedical Sciences
College Station, TX 77843
Telephone: 979-845-5051
www.cvm.tamu.edu

Virginia - Maryland

Virginia Tech
Virginia-Maryland Regional
College of Veterinary Medicine
Blacksburg, VA 24061
Telephone: 540-231-7666
www.vetmed.vt.edu

Washington

Washington State University
College of Veterinary Medicine
Pullman, WA 99164
Telephone: 509-335-9515
www.vetmed.wsu.edu

Wisconsin

University of Wisconsin-Madison
School of Veterinary Medicine
2015 Linden Drive West
Madison, WI 53706
Telephone: 608-263-6716
www.vetmed.wisc.edu

Canada - Ontario

University of Guelph
Ontario Veterinary College
Guelph, ON N1G 2W1
CANADA
Telephone: 519-824-4120
www.ovcnet.uoguelph.ca

Prince Edward Island

University of Prince Edward Island

108

Atlantic Veterinary College
550 University Avenue
Charlottetown, PE C1A 4P3
CANADA
Telephone: 902-566-0882
www.upei.ca/~avc

Québec

Université de Montréal
Faculté de Médecine Vétérinaire
C.P. 5000
Saint Hyacinthe, PQ J2S 7C6
CANADA
Telephone: 450-773-8521
www.medvet.umontreal.ca

Saskatchewan

University of Saskatchewan
Western College of Veterinary Medicine
52 Campus Drive
Saskatoon, SK S7N 5B4
CANADA
Telephone: 306-966-7447
www.usask.ca/wcvm

Australia

Murdoch University
Division of Veterinary and Biomedical Sciences
Murdoch
WESTERN AUSTRALIA
Telephone: 61 8 9360 2566
www.vet.murdoch.edu.au

The University of Melbourne
Faculty of Veterinary Science
Werribee, VIC Australia
Telephone: 61 3 9731 2261
www.vet.unimelb.edu.au

The University of Sydney
Faculty of Veterinary Science
NSW 2006
AUSTRALIA
Telephone: 61 2 9351 6936
www.vetsci.usyd.edu.au

England

University of London
The Royal Veterinary College
Royal College Street
London NW1 OTU
ENGLAND
Telephone: 44 (0)20 7468-5000
www.rvc.ac.uk

The Netherlands

State University of Utrecht
Faculty of Veterinary Medicine
PO Box 80.163
3508 TD Utrecht
THE NETHERLANDS
Telephone: 31 30 253-4851
www.vet.uu.nl

New Zealand

Massey University College of Sciences
Institute of Veterinary, Animal, and Biomedical Sciences
Palmerston North
NEW ZEALAND
Telephone: 64 6 350-5714
www.ivabs.massey.ac.nz

Scotland

University of Glasgow
Faculty of Veterinary Medicine
Glasgow, Scotland G61 1QH
Telephone: 44 (0)141 330-5700
www.gla.ac.uk/faculties/vet

The University of Edinburgh
Royal School of Veterinary Studies
Summerhall
Edinburgh EH9 1QH
SCOTLAND
Telephone: 44 131 650-1000
www.vet.ed.ac.uk

Veterinary Associations

American Veterinary Medical Association
1931 North Meacham Road, Suite 100
Schaumburg, IL 60173
Telephone: 847-925-8070
Fax: 847-925-1329
www.avma.org

Association of American Veterinary Medical Colleges
1101 Vermont Avenue, NW, Suite 301
Washington, DC 20005
Telephone: 202-371-9195
Fax: 202-842-0773
www.aavmc.org

Veterinary Medical College Application Service
(a branch of the AAVMC)
Toll Free: 877-862-2740
Fax: 202-682-1122
www.aavmc.org

Appendix II:
Veterinary Technology Programs

The following programs are listed for those students who will not pursue admission to veterinary school yet want to explore the possibility of a veterinary technology education. Being a veterinary technician is a wonderful alternative for those who do not feel that a doctoral program at a veterinary school is the right fit.

In some rare cases when a Bachelor's degree is offered, veterinary technician students may be able to pursue both a veterinary technology degree and a pre-veterinary program.

Arizona

Long Technical College
Veterinary Technology Program
13450 N. Black Canyon Hwy., Suite 104
Phoenix, AZ 85029
Telephone: 602-548-1955
www.longtechnicalcollege.com

Mesa Community College
Veterinary Technology/Animal Health Program
1833 W. Southern Avenue
Mesa, AZ 85202
Telephone: 480-461-7488
www.mc.maricopa.edu
Associate in Applied Science

Penn Foster College
Veterinary Technician Distance Education Program
14624 N. Scottsdale Road, Suite 310
Scottsdale, AZ 85254
Telephone: 800-275-4410
www.pennfostercollege.edu
Associate of Science

Pima Community College
Veterinary Technology Program
8181 E. Irvington Road
Tucson, AZ 85709-4000
Telephone: 520-206-7414
www.pima.edu
Associate in Applied Science

California

California State Polytechnic University-Pomona
College of Agriculture
Animal Health Technology Program
3801 W. Temple Ave.
Pomona, CA 91768
Telephone: 909-869-2136
www.csupomona.edu
Bachelor of Science

Cosumnes River College
Veterinary Technology Program
8401 Center Pkwy.
Sacramento, CA 95823
Telephone: 916-691-7355
www.crc.losrios.cc.ca.us
Associate in Science

Foothill College
Veterinary Technology Program
12345 El Monte RD.

Los Altos Hills, CA 94022
Telephone: 650-949-7203
www.foothill.fhda.edu
Associate in Science

Hartnell College
Animal Health Technology Program
156 Homestead Ave.
Salinas, CA 93901
Telephone: 831-755-6855
www.hartnell.cc.ca.us
Associate in Science

Los Angeles Pierce College
Veterinary Technology Program
6201 Winnetka Ave.
Woodland Hills, CA 91371
Telephone: 818-347-0551
www.macrohead.com/rvt
Associate in Science

Mt. San Antonio College
Animal Health Technology Program
1100 N. Grand Ave.
Walnut, CA 91789
Telephone: 909-594-5611
www.mtsac.edu
Associate in Science

Western Career College-Citrus Heights Campus
7301 Greenback Lane, Suite A
Citrus Heights, CA 95621
Telephone: 916-722-8200
www.westerncollege.edu
Associate in Science

Western Career College-Pleasant Hill
Veterinary Technician Program
380 Civic Drive, #300
Pleasant Hill, CA 94523
Telephone: 925-609-6650
www.westerncollege.com/
Associate in Science

Western Career College-Sacramento
Veterinary Technology Program
8909 Folsom Blvd.
Sacramento, CA 95826
Telephone: 916-361-1660
www.westerncollege.com/
Associate in Science

Western Career College-San Leandro
Veterinary Technology Program
170 Bayfair Mall
San Leandro, CA 94578
Telephone: 510-276-3888
www.westerncollege.com/
Associate in Science

Western Career College-Stockton Campus
Veterinary Technician Education Program
1313 West Robinhood Drive, Suite B
Stockton, CA 95207
Telephone: 209-956-1240
www.westerncollege.edu
Associate in Science

Yuba College
Veterinary Technology Program
2088 N. Beale Rd.
Marysville, CA 95901
Telephone: 530-741-6962
www.yccd.edu/yuba/vettech/index.html
Associate in Science

Colorado

Bel-Rea Institute of Animal Technology
1681 S. Dayton St.
Denver, CO 80231
Telephone: 800-950-8001
www.bel-rea.com
Associate in Science

Colorado Mountain College
Veterinary Technology Program
Spring Valley Campus
3000 County Rd. 114
Glenwood Springs, CO 81601

Telephone: 970-945-8691
www.coloradomtn.edu
Associate in Applied Science

Community College of Denver
Veterinary Technology Program
1070 Alton Way
Denver, CO 80230
Telephone: 303-365-8300
www.ccd.rightchoice.org
Associate in Applied Science

Front Range Community College
Veterinary Research Technology Program
4616 S. Shields
Ft. Collins, CO 80526
Telephone: 970-226-2500
www.frcc.cc.co.us
Associate in Applied Science

Connecticut

NW Connecticut Community College
Veterinary Technology Program
Park Place East
Winsted, CT 06098
Telephone: 860-738-6490
www.nwctc.commnet.edu
Associate in Science

Quinnipiac University
Veterinary Technology Program
Mt. Carmel Ave.
Hamden, CT 06518
Telephone: 203-582-8958
www.quinnipiac.edu
Bachelor of Science

Delaware

Delaware Technical and Community College
Veterinary Technology Program
PO Box 610, Route 18
Georgetown, DE 19947
Telephone: 302-855-5918
www.dtcc.edu
Associate in Applied Science

Florida

Brevard Community College
Veterinary Technology Program
1519 Clearlake Rd.
Cocoa, FL 32922
Telephone: 321-433-7594
www.brevard.cc.fl.us
Associate of Science

Miami-Dade College
Veterinary Technology Program
Medical Center Campus
950 NW 20th Street
Miami, FL 33127
Telephone: 305-237-4473
www.mdcc.edu
Associate in Science

St. Petersburg College
Veterinary Technology Program
Box 13489
St. Petersburg, FL 33733
Telephone: 727-341-3652
www.spjc.edu
Associate in Science

Georgia

Athens Technical College
Veterinary Technology Program
800 US Highway 29N
Athens, GA 30601
Telephone: 706-355-5107
www.athenstech.edu
Associate of Applied Science

Fort Valley State University
Veterinary Technology Program
1005 State University Drive
Fort Valley, GA 31030
Telephone: 478-825-6353
www.fvsu.edu/
Associate of Applied Science
Bachelor of Science

Gwinnett Technical College
Veterinary Technology Program
5150 Sugarloaf Pkwy.
Lawrenceville, GA 30043
Telephone: 770-962-7580
www.gwinnetttechnicalcollege.com
Associate of Applied Technology

Ogeechee Technical College
Veterinary Technology Program
1 Joe Kennedy Blvd.
Statesboro, GA 30458
Telephone: 912-688-6037
www.ogeecheetech.edu
Associate in Applied Science

Idaho

College of Southern Idaho
Veterinary Technology Program
315 Falls Ave.
Twin Falls, ID 83303-1238
Telephone: 208-733-9554
www.csi.cc.id.us
Associate of Applied Science

Illinois

Parkland College
Veterinary Technology Program
2400 W. Bradley Ave.
Champaign, IL 61821
Telephone: 217-351-2224
www.parkland.edu
Associate in Applied Science

Joliet Junior College
Agriculture Sciences Department
1215 Houbolt Road
Joliet, IL 60431
Telephone: 815-280-2746
www.jjc.cc.il.us
Associate in Applied Science

Indiana

Purdue University
School of Veterinary Medicine
Veterinary Technology Program
West Lafayette, IN 47907
Telephone: 765-494-7619
www.vet.purdue.edu
Associate in Applied Science
Bachelor of Science

Iowa

Des Moines Area Community College
Veterinary Technology Program
2805 SW Snyder Dr
Ankeny, IA 50023
Telephone: 800-362-2127
www.dmacc.edu
Associate of Applied Science

Kirkwood Community College
Animal Health Technology Program
6301 Kirkwood Blvd., SW
Cedar Rapids, IA 52406
Telephone: 319-398-5411
www.kirkwood.edu
Associate in Applied Science

Kansas

Colby Community College
Veterinary Technology Program
1255 S. Range
Colby, KS 67701
Telephone: 785-460-5466
www.colbycc.edu
Associate in Applied Science

Kentucky

Morehead State University
Veterinary Technology Program
25 MSU Farm Dr.
Morehead, KY 40351

Telephone: 606-783-2326
www.morehead-st.edu
Associate in Veterinary Science

Murray State University
Animal Health Technology Program
Department of Agriculture
100 AHT Center
Murray, KY 42071
Telephone: 270-762-7001
www.murraystate.edu
Bachelor in Science

Louisiana

Delgado Community College
615 City Park Avenue
New Orleans, LA 70119-4399
Telephone: 504-483-4327
www.dcc.edu
Associate in Applied Science

Northwestern State University of Louisiana
Veterinary Technology Program
225 Bienvenu Hall
Natchitoches, LA 71497
Telephone: 318-357-5323
www.nsula.edu
Associate in Science

Maine

University College of Bangor
Veterinary Technology Program
85 Texas Ave
Bangor, ME 04401-4367
Telephone: 207-262-7852
www.uma.maine.edu/bangor
Associate of Science

Maryland

Essex Campus of the Community College
Of Baltimore County
Veterinary Technology Program
7201 Rossville Blvd.

120

Baltimore, MD 21237
Telephone: 410-780-6306
www.ccbcmd.edu
Associate degree

Massachusetts

Becker College
Veterinary Technology Program
964 Main Street
Leicester, MA 01524
Telephone: 508-791-9241
www.beckercollege.com
Associate in Science
Bachelor of Science

Holyoke Community College
Veterinary Technician Program
303 Homestead Ave.
Holyoke, MA 01040
Telephone: 413-538-7000
www.hcc.mass.edu
Associate in Science

Mount Ida College
Veterinary Technology Program
777 Dedham St.
Newton, MA 02459
Telephone: 617-928-4545
www.mountida.edu
Associate in Arts
Bachelor of Science

Michigan

Baker College of Cadillac
Veterinary Technology Program
9600 East 13th Street
Cadillac, MI 49601
Telephone: 231-775-8458
www.baker.edu
Associate of Applied Science

Baker College of Flint
Veterinary Technology Program
1050 W. Bristol Road

Flint, MI 48507
Telephone: 800-964-4299
www.baker.edu
Associate of Applied Science

Baker College of Jackson
Veterinary Technology Program
2800 Springport Road
Jackson, MI 49202
Telephone: 800-937-0337
www.baker.edu
Associate in Applied Science

Baker College of Muskegon
Veterinary Technology Program
1903 Marquette Ave
Muskegon, MI 49442
Telephone: 800-937-0337
www.baker.edu
Associate of Applied Science

Macomb Community College
Veterinary Technician Program
44575 Garfield Rd.
Clinton Township, MI 48044
Telephone: 586-286-2096
www.macomb.cc.mi.us
Associate in Applied Science

Michigan State University
College of Veterinary Medicine
Veterinary Technology Program
East Lansing, MI 48824
Telephone: 517-353-7267
www.cvm.msu.edu
Associate in Applied Science
Bachelor of Science

Wayne County Community College District
Veterinary Technology Program
c/o Wayne State University
Div. of Laboratory Animal Resources
540 E. Canfield Rd.
Detroit, MI 48201
Telephone: 313-577-1156
www.dlar.wayne.edu
Associate in Applied Science

Minnesota

Argosy University-Twin City
Veterinary Technician Program
1515 Central Parkway
Eagan, MN 55121
Telephone: 888-844-2004
www.argosyu.edu
Associate in Applied Science

Duluth Business University
Veterinary Technology Program
4724 Mike Colalillo Dr.
Duluth, MN 55807
Telephone: 800-777-8406
www.dbumn.edu
Associate in Applied Science

Globe College
Veterinary Technology Program
7166 10th St North
Oakdale, MN 55128
Telephone: 800-231-0660
www.globecollege.edu
Associate of Applied Science

Minnesota School of Business-Brooklyn Center
Veterinary Technology Program
5910 Shingle Creek Parkway
Brooklyn Center, Minnesota 55430
Telephone: 763-585-5239
www.msbcollege.edu
Associate in Applied Science

Minnesota School of Business-Plymouth
Veterinary Technology Program
1455 County Road 101 North
Plymouth, MN 55447
Telephone: 763-476-2000
www.msbcollege.edu
Associate in Applied Science

Minnesota School of Business-Shakopee
Veterinary Technology Program
1200 Shakopee Town Square
Shakopee, MN 55379

Telephone: 952-345-1200
www.msbcollege.edu
Associate in Applied Science

Ridgewater College
Veterinary Technology Dept.
2101 15th Ave., NW
Willmar, MN 56201
Telephone: 320-235-5114
www.ridgewater.mnscu.edu
Associate in Applied Science

Rochester Community and Technical College
Animal Health Technology Program
851 30th Avenue SE
Rochester, MN 55904
Telephone: 800-247-1296
www.rctc.edu
Associate in Applied Science

Mississippi

Hinds Community College
Veterinary Technology Program
1100 PMB 11160
Raymond, MS 39154
Telephone: 601-857-3456
www.hindscc.edu
Associate in Applied Science

Northwest Mississippi Community College
Veterinary Technology Program
4975 Highway 51 North
Senatobia, MS 38668
Telephone: 662-562-3222
www.northwestms.edu
Associate in Applied Science

Missouri

Crowder College
601 LaClede Avenue
Neosho, MO 64850
Telephone: 417-455-5772
www.crowder.edu
Associate Degree

Jefferson College
Veterinary Technology Program
1000 Viking Dr
Hillsboro, MO 63050
Telephone: 636-942-3000
www.jeffco.edu
Associate in Applied Science

Maple Woods Community College
Veterinary Technology Program
2601 NE Barry Rd.
Kansas City, MO 64156
Telephone: 816-437-3235
www.kcmetro.edu
Associate in Applied Science

Nebraska

Nebraska College of Technical Agriculture
Veterinary Technology Program
RR3, Box 23A
Curtis, NE 69025
Telephone: 308-367-4124
www.ncta.unl.edu
Associate in Applied Science

Northeast Community College
Veterinary Technician Program
801 E. Benjamin Ave.
Norfolk, NE 68702
Telephone: 402-371-2020
www.northeastcollege.com
Associate in Applied Science

Vatterott College
Veterinary Technician Program
11818 I St
Omaha, NE 68137-1237
Telephone: 402-392-1300
www.vatterott-college.com
Associate in Applied Science

Nevada

Community College of Southern Nevada
Veterinary Technology Program

6375 W. Charleston Blvd.
Las Vegas, NV 89146
Telephone: 702-651-5852
www.ccsn.nevada.edu
Associate in Applied Science

Pima Medical Institute
Veterinary Technician Program
3333 E. Flamingo Road
Las Vegas, NV 89121
Telephone: 702-458-9650
www.pmi.edu
Occupational Associate

Truckee Meadows Community College
Veterinary Technology Program
7000 Dandini Blvd.
Reno, NV 89512
Telephone: 775-850-4005
www.tmcc.edu
Associate in Science

New Hampshire

New Hampshire Community Technical College
Veterinary Technology Program
277 Portsmouth Ave.
Stratham, NH 03885
Telephone: 603-772-1194
www.nhctc.edu
Associate in Science

New Jersey

Camden County College
Animal Science Technology Program
P.O. Box 200
Blackwood, NJ 08012
Telephone: 856-227-7200
www.camdencc.edu
Associate in Applied Science

Northern New Jersey Consortium for
Veterinary Technician Education
400 Paramus Road
Paramus, NJ 07652

126

Telephone: 201-612-5389
www.bergen.cc.nj.us
Associate in Applied Science

New Mexico

Central New Mexico Community College
Veterinary Technology Program
525 Buena Vista SE
Albuquerque, NM 87106
Telephone: 505-224-5043
www.cnm.edu
Associate in Applied Science

New York

Alfred State College
Veterinary Technology Program
Agriculture Science Building
Alfred, NY 14801
Telephone: 607-578-3009
www.alfredstate.edu
Associate in Applied Science

La Guardia Community College, CUNY
Veterinary Technology Program
31-10 Thomson Ave.
Long Island City, NY 11101
Telephone: 718-482-5470
www.lagcc.cuny.edu
Associate in Applied Science

Medaille College
Veterinary Technology Program
18 Agassiz Ct
Buffalo, NY 14214
Telephone: 716-884-3281
www.medaille.edu
Associate in Science

Mercy College
Veterinary Technology Program
555 Broadway
Dobbs Ferry, NY 10522
Telephone: 914-674-7530
www.mercy.edu
Bachelor of Science

State University of New York-Canton
Agricultural & Technical College
Veterinary Science Technology Program
34 Cornell Drive
Canton, NY 13617
Telephone: 315-386-7410
www.canton.edu
Associate in Applied Science

State University of New York-Delhi
College of Technology
Veterinary Science Technology Program
156 Farnsworth Hall
Delhi, NY 13753
Telephone: 607-746-4306
www.delhi.edu
Associate in Applied Science
Bachelor in Business Administration

Ulster County Community College
Veterinary Technology Program
Cottekill Road
Stone Ridge, NY 12484
Telephone: 800-724-0833
www.sunyulster.edu
Associate in Applied Science

Suffolk Community College
Veterinary Science Technology Program
Western Campus
Crooked Hill Rd.
Brentwood, NY 11717
Telephone: 631-851-6289
www.sunysuffolk.edu
Associate in Applied Science

North Carolina

Asheville-Buncombe Technical Community College
Veterinary Medical Technology Program
340 Victoria Road
Asheville, NC 28801
Telephone: 828-254-1921
www.abtech.edu
Associate in Applied Science

Central Carolina Community College
Veterinary Medical Technology Program
1105 Kelly Dr.
Sanford, NC 27330
Telephone: 919-775-5401
www.ccarolina.cc.nc.us
Associate in Applied Science

Gaston College
Veterinary Medical Technology Program
201 Hwy. 321 South
Dallas, NC 28034-1499
Telephone: 704-922-6200
www.gaston.cc.nc.us
Associate in Applied Science

North Dakota

North Dakota State University
Veterinary Technology Program
Van Es Laboratories
Fargo, ND 58105
Telephone: 701-231-7511
www.ndsu.nodak.edu
Bachelor of Science

Ohio

Columbus State Community College
Veterinary Technology Program
550 E. Spring St.
Columbus, OH 43216
Telephone: 614-287-3685
www.cscc.edu
Associate in Applied Science

Cuyahoga Community College
Veterinary Technology Program
11000 Pleasant Valley Rd.
Parma, OH 44130
Telephone: 216-987-5450
www.tri-c.cc.oh.us
Associate of Applied Science

UC Raymond Walters College
Veterinary Technology Program

9555 Plainfield Road
Blue Ash, OH 45236
Telephone: 513-936-7173
www.rwc.uc.edu
Associate of Applied Science

Stautzenberger College
Veterinary Technology Program
5355 Southwyck Blvd.
Toledo, OH 43614
Telephone: 419-866-0261
www.stautzen.com
Associate in Applied Science

Vet Tech Institute at Bradford School
2469 Stelzer Road
Columbus, OH 43219
Telephone: 614-416-6200
www.bradfordschoolcolumbus.edu
Associate in Applied Science

Oklahoma

Murray State College
Veterinary Technology Program
One Murray Campus
Tishomingo, OK 73460
Telephone: 580-371-2371
www.msc.cc.ok.us
Associate in Applied Science

Oklahoma State University - Oklahoma City
Veterinary Technology Program
900 N. Portland Ave.
Oklahoma City, OK 73107
Telephone: 405-945-9112
www.osuokc.edu
Associate in Applied Science

Tulsa Community College
Veterinary Technology Program
7505 W. 41st St.
Tulsa, OK 74107
Telephone: 918-595-8214
www.tulsa.cc.ok.us
Associate in Applied Science)

Oregon

Portland Community College
Veterinary Technology Program
P.O. Box 19000
Portland, OR 97219
Telephone: 503-244-6111
www.pcc.edu
Associate in Applied Science

Pennsylvania

Harcum College
Veterinary Technology Program
750 Montgomery Ave.
Bryn Mawr, PA 19010-3476
Telephone: 610-526-6055
www.harcum.edu
Associate in Science

Johnson College
Veterinary Science Technology Program
3427 N. Main Ave.
Scranton, PA 18508
Telephone: 570-342-6404
www.johnsoncollege.com
Associate in Science

Lehigh Carbon & Northampton Community Colleges
Veterinary Technology Program
3835 Green Pond Rd.
Bethlehem, PA 18020
Telephone: 610-861-5548
www.lccc.edu
Associate of Applied Science

Manor College
Veterinary Technology Program
700 Fox Chase Road
Jenkintown, PA 19046
Telephone: 215-885-2360
www.manorvettech.com
Associate in Science

The Vet Tech Institute
Veterinary Technician Program
125 Seventh Street
Pittsburgh, PA 15222
Telephone: 800-570-0693
www.vettechinstitute.com
Associate in Specialized Technology

Western School of Health and Business Careers
Veterinary Technology Program
421 7th Avenue
Pittsburgh, PA 15219
Telephone: 412-281-2600
www.westernschool.com
Associate in Specialized Technology

Wilson College
Veterinary Medical Technology Program
1015 Philadelphia Ave.
Chambersburg, PA 17201
Telephone: 717-264-4141
www.wilson.edu
Bachelor of Science

South Carolina

Newberry College
Veterinary Technology Program
2100 College St.
Newberry, SC 29108
Telephone: 803-321-5262
www.newberry.edu
Bachelor of Science

Tri-County Technical College
Veterinary Technology Program
P.O. Box 587
Pendleton, SC 29670
Telephone: 864-646-8361
www.tctc.edu
Associate in Health Science

Trident Technical College
Veterinary Technology Program
1001 South Live Oak Drive
Moncks Corner, SC 29461

Telephone: 843-899-8011
www.tridenttech.edu
Associate in Allied Health Sciences

South Dakota

National American University
Veterinary Technology Program
321 Kansas City St.
Rapid City, SD 57701
Telephone: 800-843-8892
www.national.edu
Associate in Applied Science

Tennessee

Columbia State Community College
Veterinary Technology Program
P.O. Box 1315
Columbia, TN 38401
Telephone: 931-540-2722
www.coscc.cc.tn.us
Associate in Applied Science

Lincoln Memorial University
Veterinary Technology Program
Cumberland Gap Pkwy.
Harrogate, TN 37752
Telephone: 423-869-6278
www.lmunet.edu
Associate in Science
Bachelor of Science

Texas

Dallas County Community College District
Cedar Valley College
Veterinary Technology Program
3030 N. Dallas Ave.
Lancaster, TX 75134
Telephone: 972-860-8127
www.dcccd.edu
Associate in Applied Science

McLennan Community College
Veterinary Technology Program

1400 College Drive
Waco, TX 76708
Telephone: 254-299-8750
www.mclennan.edu
Associate in Applied Science

Midland College
Veterinary Technology Program
3600 N. Garfield
Midland, TX 79705
Telephone: 432-685-4619
www.midland.edu
Associate in Applied Science

Alamo Community College District
Palo Alto College
Veterinary Technology Program
1400 W. Villaret Blvd.
San Antonio, TX 78224
Telephone: 210-531-8709
www.accd.edu
Associate of Applied Science

Sul Ross State University
School of Agriculture & Natural Resource Sciences
Veterinary Technology Program
P.O. Box C-114
Alpine, TX 79830
Telephone: 432-837-8205
www.sulross.edu
Associate Degree

Tomball College
Veterinary Technology Program
30555 Tomball Pkwy.
Tomball, TX 77375
Telephone: 281-351-3357
www.tc.nhmccd.cc.tx.us
Associate in Applied Science

Utah

Utah Career College
Veterinary Technician Program
1902 West 7800 South
West Jordan, UT 84088

134

Telephone: 801-676-0237
www.utahcollege.com
Associate in Applied Science

Vermont

Vermont Technical College
Veterinary Technology Program
Randolph Center, VT 05061
Telephone: 802-728-3391
www.vtc.vsc.edu
Associate in Applied Science

Virginia

Blue Ridge Community College
Veterinary Technology Program
Box 80
Weyers Cave, VA 24486
Telephone: 540-234-9261
www.br.cc.va.us
Associate in Science

Northern Virginia Community College
Veterinary Technology Program
Loudoun Campus
1000 Harry Flood Byrd Hwy.
Sterling, VA 20164-8699
Telephone: 703-450-2525
www.nv.cc.va.us
Associate in Applied Science

Washington

Pierce College Ft. Steilacoom
Veterinary Technology Program
9401 Farwest Dr., SW
Lakewood, WA 98498
Telephone: 253-964-6668
www.pierce.ctc.edu
Associate in Animal Technology

Yakima Valley Community College
Veterinary Technology Program
P.O. Box 22520
Yakima, WA 98907

Telephone: 509-574-4759
www.yvcc.cc.wa.us
Associate of Applied Science

West Virginia

Pierpont Community & Technical College
Veterinary Technology Program
1201 Locust Ave.
Fairmont, WV 26554
Telephone: 304-367-4589
www.fscwv.edu
Associate in Applied Science

Wisconsin

Madison Area Technical College
Veterinary Technician Program
3550 Anderson
Madison, WI 53704
Telephone: 608-246-6100
www.madison.tec.wi.us
Associate in Applied Science

Wyoming

Eastern Wyoming College
Veterinary Technology Program
3200 W. C St.
Torrington, WY 82240
Telephone: 800-658-3195
www.ewc.wy.edu
Associate in Applied Science

Puerto Rico

University of Puerto Rico
Veterinary Technology Program
Medical Sciences Campus
P.O. Box 365067
San Juan, PR 00936
Telephone: 787-758-2525
www.cprsweb.rcm.upr.edu
Bachelor of Science

Appendix III:
Animal and Veterinary Organizations

The following list of organizations demonstrates the breadth and depth of the veterinary profession. You may discover by browsing this list that there is a local organization near you that may be of interest to you. You may even be able to acquire some animal and/or veterinary experience at some of these organizations. All of these organizations have websites. To learn more about these organizations, type the name of the organization into an Internet search engine. (The list is not intended to be an all-inclusive list of animal and veterinary organization.)

Academy of Veterinary Allergy & Clinical Immunology
Academy of Veterinary Emergency & Critical Care Technicians
Academy of Veterinary Homeopathy
Activists of Delaware Valley Animal Network
Adopt a Greyhound
Adopt-A-Greyhound of Central Canada
Akbash Dogs International Rescue Service
Alaska Raptor Rehabilitation Center
Alberta's At-Risk Wildlife
All Creatures Animal Caring Society
Alpha Psi Veterinary Fraternity, Alpha Chapter - Ohio State University CVM
Alpha Psi Veterinary Fraternity, Pi Chapter - Virginia - Maryland CVM

Alpha Psi Veterinary Fraternity, Sigma Chapter - University of Tennessee CVM
Alternative Medicine Our Undeniable Right
Alternatives to Animal Testing Bibliography
American Academy of Veterinary Informatics
American Academy of Veterinary Pharmacology and Therapeutics
American Animal Hospital Association
American Association for Laboratory Animal Science
American Association of Bovine Practitioners
American Association of Electrodiagnostic Medicine
American Association of Equine Practitioners
American Association of Feline Practitioners
American Association of Pharmaceutical Scientists
American Association of Public Health Veterinarians
American Association of Swine Practitioners
American Association of Veterinary Anatomists
American Association of Veterinary Clinicians
American Association of Veterinary Immunologists
American Association of Veterinary Laboratory Diagnosticians
American Association of Veterinary Medical Colleges
American Association of Veterinary Parasitologists
American Association of Veterinary State Boards
American Association of Wildlife Veterinarians
American Association of Zoo Veterinarians
American Association of Zookeepers
American Biological Safety Association
American Board of Veterinary Toxicology
American Boarding Kennels Association
American Canine Sports Medicine Association
American College of Laboratory Animal Medicine
American College of Theriogenologists
American College of Veterinary Anesthesiologists
American College of Veterinary Clinical Pharmacology
American College of Veterinary Internal Medicine
American College of Veterinary Microbiologists
American College of Veterinary Ophthalmologists
American College of Veterinary Pathologists
American College of Veterinary Preventive Medicine
American College of Veterinary Radiology
American College of Veterinary Surgeons
American Committee on Laboratory Animal Diseases
American Council on Science and Health
American Dairy Goat Association
American Dairy Science Association
American Egg Board

American Fancy Rat and Mouse Association
American Farm Bureau Federation
American Federation of Aviculture
American Feed Industry Association
American Ferret Association
American Fisheries Society
American Humane Association
American Humane Association
American Institute of Fisheries Research Biologists
American Jersey Cattle Association
American Kennel Club
American Meat Institute
American Meat Science Association
American Medical Informatics Association
American Morgan Horse Association
American National Standards Institute
American Ornithologists' Union
American Ostrich Association
American Pet Association, Inc.
American Pet Products Manufacturers Association
American Physiological Society
American Pomeranian Club Breed Rescue
American Pre-Veterinary Medical Association
American Public Health Association
American Quarter Horse Association
American Saddlebred Horse Association
American Sheep Industry Association
American Society for Cell Biology
American Society for Microbiology
American Society for Nutritional Sciences
American Society for Pharmacology and Experimental Therapeutics
American Society for the Prevention of Cruelty to Animals
American Society for Virology
American Society of Agricultural Engineers
American Society of Animal Science
American Society of Ichthyologists and Herpetologists
American Society of Laboratory Animal Practitioners
American Society of Mammalogists
American Society of Parasitologists
American Society of Primatologists
American Society of Tropical Medicine and Hygiene
American Society of Veterinary Ophthalmology
American Tortoise Rescue
American Veterinary Chiropractic Association
American Veterinary Dental College

American Veterinary Distributors Association
American Veterinary Medical Association
American Veterinary Medical Foundation
American Zoo and Aquarium Association
Americans for Medical Progress
Animal Aid
Animal Alliance of Canada
Animal Ark
Animal Behavior and Welfare Sites
Animal Behavior Society
Animal Cruelty Investigation Unit
Animal Emancipation, Inc.
Animal Friends Inc. (Pittsburgh, PA)
Animal Health Distributors Association
Animal Health Information Specialists
Animal Health Institute
Animal Health/Emerging Animal Diseases
Animal Home
Animal Humane Society of Hennepin County, MN
Animal Industry Foundation
Animal Legal Defense Fund
Animal Liberation Action Group - University of Wisconsin Oshkosh
Animal Liberation Frontline Information Service
Animal Liberation Victoria
Animal People
Animal Productivity and Health Information Network – U. of Prince Edward Island
Animal Protective League
Animal Protesters' Bulletin
Animal Rescue Kingdom
Animal Rescue League of Boston
Animal Rescue League of Iowa, Inc.
Animal Research Data Base
Animal Responsibility Cyprus
Animal Rights FAQ
Animal Rights Foundation of Florida
Animal Rights Hawaii
Animal Rights Law Center,Rutgers University
Animal Rights News
Animal Rights Resource Site
Animal Trustees of Austin, Inc.
Animal Welfare Institute
Animal-Assisted-Therapy-Team
AnimaLife
Animaline Rescue

140

Animals At Risk Care Sanctuary Home Page
Animals Unlimited, Inc.
Anne Arundel County SPCA
Applied Research Ethics National Association
Aquatic Conservation Network
ARK Online
Association for Assessment and Accreditation of Laboratory Animal Care
Association for Biology Laboratory Education
Association for Gnotobiotics
Association for Research in Vision and Ophthalmology
Association for the Study of Animal Behavior
Association for Veterinary Clinical Pharmacology and Therapeutics
Association for Veterinary Informatics
Association of American Feed Control Officials
Association of Avian Veterinarians
Association of Field Ornithologists
Association of Food and Drug Officials
Association of Pet Behavior Counselors
Association of Reptilian & Amphibian Veterinarians
Association of Veterinarians for Animal Rights
Association of Veterinarians for Animal Rights
Association of Veterinary Anaesthetists
Association of Veterinary Students
Athens Alliance of Allbreed Canine Rescue
Atlantic Salmon Federation
Auburn University Pre-Veterinary Medical Association
Audubon in New York
Auxiliary to the AVMA
AVMA Network of Animal Health
Bat Conservation International
Bay Area Siberian Husky Rescue Referral
Bear Watch
Beauty without Cruelty India
Because You Care (Erie County, PA)
Berkeley County Humane Society (West Virginia)
Bide-A-Wee Home Association
Biodiversity Conservation Center-West
Biodiversity Forum
Biomedical Research Education Trust
Body Shop
Border Collie Rescue
Boxer Rescue, USA
Brazos Valley Animal Shelter (Texas)
Bristol Exotic and Wild Animal Society

Bull Pages - Rainforest Information Links Page
C.L. Davis Foundation for the Advancement of Veterinary and Comparative Pathology
California Biomedical Research Association
California Domestic Ferret Association
Canadian Association for Laboratory Animal Science
Canadian Association of Animal Breeders
Canadian Association of Veterinary Ophthalmology
Canadian Council on Animal Care
Canadian Federation of Humane Societies
Canadian Nature Federation
Canadian Pork Council
Canadian Swine Breeders Association
Canadian Veterinary Medical Association
Canadian World Parrot Trust
Candy Kitchen Rescue Ranch
Canine Companions for Independence
Canine Eye Registration Foundation
Care for the Wild
Carnivore Preservation Trust
Carolina Raptor Center
Cat Fancier's Association
Cat Network (St. Louis, MO)
Cats Haven (Indianapolis, IN)
Cats Protection League
Cat's Voice
Celia Hammond Animal Trust
Center for Animal Alternatives (University of California-Davis)
Center for Conservation Biology
Cetacean Society International
Chameleon Conservation Society
Champaign County Humane Society
Cheetah Survival Page
Chemical Industry Institute of Toxicology
Chicago House Rabbit Society
Christian Veterinary Mission
Christian Veterinary Missions of Canada
College of Veterinarians of Ontario
Colorado Herpetological Society
Colorado Horse Rescue
Colorado Natural Heritage Program
Commonwealth Veterinary Association
Companion Animal Rescue Effort (California)
Companion Greyhounds, Inc.
Compassion in World Farming
Computer-aided Learning in Veterinary Education

Conference of Research Workers in Animal Diseases
Connecticut Cat Rescue Web
Connecticut United for Research Excellence
Conservation Breeding Specialist Group
Conservation Breeding Specialist Group
Consortium of Aquariums Universities & Zoos
Consortium of North American Veterinary Interactive New Concept Education
Continental Kennel Club
Cornell Research Foundation, Inc.
Council for Agricultural Science and Technology
Council of Docked Breeds
Council on Licensure, Enforcement and Regulation
Cow Liberation Front
Crustacean Society
Dairy Management Inc.
Dallas/Ft. Worth Sheltie Rescue
Darwinian Notions
Days End Farm Horse Rescue
Defenders of Wildlife
Delaware Humane Association
Delaware Veterinary Medical Association
Delta Society
Denver Dumb Friends League (CO)
Dian Fossey Gorilla Fund
Ding Darling Wildlife Society
Doberman Rescue of North Texas
Doggy Paws Rescue/Retrieval Page
Dogs in Canada Needing Homes
Dolphin Alliance
Donkey Sanctuary
Doris Day Animal League
DragonRidge Net-Refuge of the Rhino
Dreampower Animal Rescue Foundation
EarthCare
Earthkind
Earthtrust Wildlife Conservation Worldwide
East Texas Herpetological Society
Einstein's Online Pet Rescue Group
Elephant Consultancy
Elephant Manager's Association
Elmbrook Humane Society (WI)
Endangered Wildlife Trust
Endocrine Society
English Shepherd Rescue
Entomological Society of America

Ethics and Animals
Ethics Updates Animal Rights
Exotics Sanctuary
Exploits Valley SPCA (Canada)
FARM - Farm Animal Reform Movement
Farm Sanctuary
Federation of American Societies for Experimental Biology
Feline Refuge (Mt. Pleasant, SC)
Feminists for Animal Rights
Feral Cat Coalition
Ferret Home Rescue and Adoption Shelter
Ferret Wise Rescue/Rehabilitation Shelter
Finnish Veterinary Association
Florida Veterinary Medical Association
Food & Drug Law Institute
Food Animal Practitioners Club (Ohio State University)
Foundation for Biomedical Research
Frederick County Humane Society (Maryland)
Frieda's Cat Shelter (Michigan City, IN)
Friends for Life
Friends of Animals Foundation (CA)
Friends of Pets (Ohio)
Friends of the Asian Elephant
Friends of the Environment
Friends of the Sea Otter
Fund for Animals
Fund for the Replacement of Animals in Medical Experiments
Furry Friends Pet Assisted Therapy Services
Georgia Equine Rescue League, Ltd.
German Shorthaired Pointer Rescue
Global Action in Interest of Animals
Goat Veterinary Society
Golden Endings - Golden Retriever Rescue
Golden Gate English Springer Spaniel Rescue
Golden Retriever Rescue of Atlanta
Golden Retriever Rescue, Education and Training (GRREAT)
Gordon Setter Rescue
Gorilla Foundation
Gorilla Haven
Great Dane Rescue Links
Greek Animal Rescue
GreenLife Society - North America
Greenpeace International
Greyhound Companions
Greyhound Friends
Greyhound Rescue Group

144

Greyhounds Anonymous
Guide Dog Foundation for the Blind
Gulf Coast Veterinary Education Foundation
Hawk Cliff Foundation
HawkWatch International
Hayward Animal Shelter (California)
Heart Bandits - American Eskimo Dog Rescue
Heartland Humane Society (Corvallis, OR)
Herpetologist's League
High North Alliance
Hollydogs Greyhound Adoption
Homeless Cat Network
Hooved Animal Humane Society
Horse Power Projects Inc.
Houston Audubon Society
Houston Homeless Pet Placement League
Human-Animal Bond Association of Canada
Humane Innovations and Alternatives
Humane Services of Metro Atlanta
Humane Society of Boulder Valley (Colorado)
Humane Society of Clifton, CO
Humane Society of Fairfax County (Virginia)
Humane Society of Missouri
Humane Society of Ottawa Carleton (Canada)
Humane Society of Ramsey County (Minnesota)
Humane Society of Rochester and Monroe County (New York)
Humane Society of Santa Clara Valley (California)
Humane Society of the Ozarks
Humane Society of the United States
Humane Society of Tucson
Humane Society of Utah
Humanities Organization for Animal and Nature protection
Hunt Saboteurs Association
Idaho Humane Society
In Defense of Animals
Indiana Veterinary Medical Association
Industrial in Vitro Toxicology Group
Infectious Diseases Society of America
Information on Animal Alternatives Database
Institute for International Cooperation in Animal Biologics
Institute for Laboratory Animal Research
Institute of Animal Technology
Institute of International Health
Institutional Animal Care and Use Committees Page
International Academy of Compounding Pharmacists
International Arabian Horse Association

International Association for the Study of Pain
International Association of Agricultural Students
International Association of Equine Practitioners
International Association of Fish and Wildlife Agencies
International Association of Fish and Wildlife Agencies
International Aviculturists Society
International Aviculturists Society
International Center for Aquaculture and Aquatic Environments
International Council for Laboratory Animal Science
International Crane Foundation
International Federation of Placental Associations
International Fund for Animal Welfare
International Generic Horse Association / Horse Aid
International Marine Mammal Association
International Marine life Alliance
International Meat and Poultry HACCP Alliance
International Primate Protection League
International Primatological Society
International Rhino Foundation
International Society for Animal Genetics
International Society for Anthrozoology
International Society for Endangered Cats
International Society of Veterinary Perinatology
International Union of Toxicology
International Venomous Snake Society
International Veterinary Acupuncture Society
International Veterinary Biosafety Working Group
International Veterinary Students Association
International Wildlife Coalition
International Wildlife Education & Conservation
Internet Law Library: Legal Treatment of Animals
Internet Zoological Society
Iowa Raptor Foundation
Island Nature Trust
IUCN Cat Specialist Group
Jazz purr Cat Care Society (Canada)
Jews for Animal Rights
Johns Hopkins Center for Alternatives to Animal Testing
Join Hands
Journal of Applied Animal Welfare Science
K9 Haven - SF Bay Area Small Breed Rescue
Kansas Animal Welfare Information Collection
Kansas City Pet Adoption League
Kansas Veterinary Medical Association
Kenosha County (WI) Humane Society
Kentucky Humane Society

146

Kentucky Veterinary Medical Association
Kern crest Audubon Society
KittiCat.Com Feline Rescue Website
Kitty Love (Scottsdale, AZ)
Kitty Village (Atlanta, GA)
Klee Kai National Kennel Club and Rescue
Kuvasz Rescue
Kyler Laird's Animal Rescue Resources
Lab Rescue (Golden Gate Labrador Retriever Club)
Laboratory Animal Science Association
Laboratory Animal Welfare Training Exchange
Labrador Retriever Rescue Contacts
Labrador Retriever Rescue, Inc
Labrador-L Emergency Medical Assistance
Last Chance for Animals
Latham Foundation
Law Student Animal Rights Alliance
League Against Cruel Sports
League for Animal Welfare
Lepidopterists' Society
Lincolnshire Trust for Nature Conservation
Little Shelter Animal Rescue (NY)
Livestock Behavior, Facility Design and Humane Slaughter
Livestock Conservation Institute
Living Free Animal Sanctuary (Mountain Center, CA)
London Animal Action
Los Angeles SPCA
Mahale Wildlife Conservation Society
Maine Veterinary Medical Association
Make Peace with Animals
Malaria Foundation
Mammal Society
Mammary Gland Physiology and Pathology Society
Manx Nature Conservation Trust
Mare & Foal Sanctuary
Marin Humane Society
Maryland Veterinary Medical Association
Maryland Veterinary Medical Association
Massachusetts Society for Medical Research
Massachusetts Society for the Prevention of Cruelty to Animals
Springfield Animal Shelter
Massachusetts Veterinary Medical Association
Massey University Veterinary Student Association
Maumee Valley Save-A-Pet (Toledo, OH)
Maxfund Animal Adoption Center (Denver, CO)
Memphis-Shelby County Veterinary Medical Association

Mercy Rescue Net
Merrimack River Feline Rescue Society
Miami (OH) University Pre-Vet Club
Michigan Animal Rescue League
Michigan Greyhound Connection
Mid-Continent Association for Agriculture, Biomedical Research and Education
Milford, MA Humane Society
Minnesota Veterinary Medical Association
MISMR - Michigan Society for Medical Research
Missing and Found Animal Pages (USDA - APHIS)
Mississippi Animal Rescue League
Monmouth County SPCA (New Jersey)
Montgomery County Society for the Prevention of Cruelty to Animals
Morris Animal Foundation
Nashville Humane Association
National 4-H Council
National Alternative Livestock Association
National Animal Interest Alliance
National Animal Poison Control Center
National Anti-Hunt Campaign
National Anti-Vivisection Society
National Association for Biomedical Research
National Association of Animal Breeders
National Association of Professional Pet Sitters
National Association of State Departments of Agriculture
National Audubon Society
National Audubon Society
National Bison Association
National Cattlemen's Beef Association
National Contract Poultry Growers Association
National Dairy Herd Improvement Association
National Farmers Organization
National Farmers Union
National Fisheries Institute
National Foundation for Infectious Diseases
National Institute for Control of Veterinary Bioproducts and Pharmaceuticals
National Livestock Producers Association
National Mastitis Council
National Meat Association
National Milk Producers Federation
National Parks and Conservation Association
National Pedigreed Livestock Council
National Pork Producers Council

148

National Society for Histotechnology
National Turkey Federation
National Turtle and Tortoise Society
National Wildlife Federation
Native Fish Society
Natural Resources Defense Council
Nature Conservancy
Nature Conservancy of Hawaii
Naturenet
Nebraska Humane Society
Neponset Valley Humane Society (Massachusetts)
New Hampshire Doberman Rescue League
New Hampshire Equine Humane Association
New Hampshire Society for the Prevention of Cruelty to Animals
New Mexico Veterinary Medical Association
New Mexico Wildlife Association
New York State House Rabbit Society
Newfoundland Rescue Links and Information
Noah's Arc (TN)
Noah's Ark Animal Foundation
Noah's Ark Rehabilitation Center (Locust Grove, GA)
NORINA Database (Audiovisual Alternatives to Laboratory Animals in Teaching)
North American Border Collie Rescue Network
North American Equine Ranching Information Council
North American Native Fishes Association
North American Vegetarian Society
North American Veterinary College Administrators
North American Veterinary Technician Association
North Carolina State University Pre-Vet Club
North Carolina Veterinary Medical Association
North Shore Animal League (New York)
North Texas Weimaraner Club - Rescue
North Valley Veterinary Technician Association
Northampton County, PA SPCA
Norwegian Reference Centre for Laboratory Animal Science & Alternatives
Nova Scotia Bird Society
Ocean Voice International
Omega Tau Sigma Veterinary Fraternity, Eta Chapter (University of Georgia)
Omega Tau Sigma Veterinary Fraternity, Iota Chapter (Oklahoma State University)
Omega Tau Sigma Veterinary Fraternity, Nu Chapter (Texas A&M University)

Omega Tau Sigma Veterinary Fraternity, Omicron Chapter (Michigan State University)
Omega Tau Sigma Veterinary Fraternity, Pi Chapter (Tuskegee University)
Omega Tau Sigma Veterinary Fraternity, Theta Chapter (University of Illinois)
Omega Tau Sigma Veterinary Fraternity, Zeta Chapter (Auburn University)
Ontario Association of Veterinary Technicians
Ontario Veterinary Medical Association
Open Your Heart (NJ)
Operation Kindness No Kill Animal Shelter (Carrollton, TX)
Oregon Biomedical Research Association
Oregon Humane Society
Oregon State University Pre-Veterinary Society
Organization of Biological Field Stations
Orlando Humane Society/SPCA of Central Florida
Ornithology and Nature Conservation in the Balearic Islands
Orphaned Wildlife Rehabilitation Society
Orthopedic Foundation for Animals
Orthopterists' Society
Pacific Rivers Council
Pat's Pet Page
PawSafe Animal Rescue
Peninsula Humane Society (San Mateo, CA)
Pennsylvania Ferret Rescue Association
Pennsylvania Society for Biomedical Research
Pennsylvania State University Pre-Veterinary Club
People Against Chimpanzee Experiments
Performing Animal Welfare Society
Pet Action League (Central Florida)
Pet Adoption (Mining Company)
Pet Adoption Fund (Canoga Park, CA)
Pet Connection (Blount County Eastern Tennessee)
Pet Industry Joint Advisory Council
Pet Place Television Show
PETA Online
Petcare Information and Advisory Service (Australia)
PetLine Lost & Found Service
PetNet, A Network of Animal Shelters
Pets Are Wonderful Support
Pets in Need (Redwood City, CA)
Pets Online
Pets Scoop
PetWhere Animal Tracking Software
Pharmachem Online

150

PhillyPAWS
Pigs Sanctuary
Pinellas Animal Foundation
Pisces
Placer County SPCA (CA)
Poultry Science Association
Pound Rescue of Athens Ohio
Predator Defense Institute
Primarily Primates
Primate Information Center
Primate Society of Great Britain
Primate Supply Information Clearinghouse
Progressive Animal Welfare Society (Washington)
Project BREED (Breed Rescue Efforts and Education)
Project Equus
Protectors of Animals, Inc. (CT)
Protesters Animal Information Network
Psychologists for the Ethical Treatment of Animals
Public Responsibility in Medicine and Research
Purrfect Pals Cat Shelter
R.E.S.C.U.E (Maricopa County - AZ)
Radiological Society of North America
Ragdoll Cat Rescue
Ranger's Realtime Rescue
Raptor Repertoire
Raptor Research Foundation, Inc.
Rat and Mouse Club of America
Registry of Comparative Pathology
Registry of Comparative Pathology
Rescue A Shar-Pei (Illinois/Indiana)
Research Defense Society
Respect for Animals
Rhode Island Veterinary Medical Association
Richmond SPCA (Virginia)
Rocky Mountain Animal Defense
Rottweiler Rescue of Mid-Michigan
Rottweilers Needing Homes
Safari Club International
San Diego Animal Advocates
San Diego County Animal Shelters
San Francisco SPCA
San Luis Obispo Animal Requesting Friends (California)
Sanctuary for Animals (Westtown, NY)
Santa Barbara Wildlife Care Network
Save a Sato
Save Our Critters Society (Washington)

Save our Squirrel Glider Possum
Save The Horse, Inc.
Save the Manatee Club
Save the Rhino International
Saving Berries for the Bears
Scientists' Center for Animal Welfare
Second Chance Pet Adoptions (North Carolina)
Shea Park - Safe Haven for Endangered Animals Exotic Animal Sanctuary
Sierra Club
Silver Lake Animal Rescue League (MI)
Society and Animals
Society for Conservation Biology (University of Texas Austin)
Society for Cryobiology
Society for In Vitro Biology
Society for Integrative and Comparative Biology
Society for the Study of Amphibians and Reptiles
Society for the Study of Amphibians and Reptiles
Society for the Study of Reproduction
Society for Theriogenology
Society for Tropical Veterinary Medicine
Society for Veterinary Medical Ethics
Society of Environmental Toxicology and Chemistry
Society of Marine Mammalogists
Society of Practicing Veterinary Surgeons
Society of Protozoologists
Society of Toxicologic Pathologists
Society of Toxicology
Somali & Abysinnian Breed Rescue & Education
SOS Rhino
Sources of Support for Research on Alternatives to Animal Use in Research and Testing
South Plains Wildlife Rehabilitation Center, Inc.
Southampton Animal Control (New York)
Southeastern Raptor Rehabilitation Center (Auburn University)
Southwest Foundation for Biomedical Research
Spay Day USA
SPCA of Anne Arundel County (Maryland)
SPCA of Texas
St. Francis Wildlife
St. Johns County Audubon Society
Standard Schnauzer Club Rescue
Stanley Park Ecology Society (Vancouver, BC)
Strays Halfway House
Street Cats Rescue Society of Alberta (Canada)
Student Organization for Animal Rights (University of Minnesota)

Student Veterinary Emergency and Critical Care Society
Student Veterinary Zoological Information Exchange
Students for Animal Liberation
Students for the Ethical Treatment of Animals (MIT)
Suffolk County, New York SPCA
Suncoast Bulldog Friends
Suncoast Seabird Sanctuary
Tarrant County Purebred Cat Rescue - Dallas/Ft. Worth Texas
Teaming With Wildlife
Tennessee Equine Veterinary Research Organization
Teratology Society
Texas A&M University Pre-Vet Society
Texas Dairy Herd Improvement Association
Texas Pet Bird Rescue
Texas Veterinary Medical Association
Three "R's" of Animal Testing Alternatives
Tiger Missing Link
Toronto Vegetarian Association
TreeHouse Animal Foundation
Tri-County Collie Rescue (MI)
Tri-Valley Animal Rescue (California)
Trojan Horse of Animal Protectionism
Trout Unlimited Canada
Turpentine Creek Exotic Wildlife Refuge
U.S. Pharmacopeia
Union of Concerned Scientists
United Egg Producers
United Poultry Concerns
United States Animal Health Association
United States Dressage Federation
Universities Federation for Animal Welfare
University of Connecticut PreVet Club
University of Florida Pre-Veterinary Medicine Club
University of Kentucky Equine Research Foundation
University of Minnesota Raptor Center
University of Missouri Pre-Veterinary Medicine Club
University of Nebraska Lincoln Pre-Veterinary Club
University of Oklahoma Pre-Vet Club
University of Rochester Pre-Veterinary Society
University of Texas at Austin Pre-Veterinary Association
University of Toronto Students for the Ethical Treatment of Animals
University of Wisconsin-Madison Pre-Veterinary Association
University of Wisconsin-River Falls PreVet Club
Upper Valley Humane Society (NH)
USA DOG (Defenders of Greyhounds)

USDA-NAL Animal Welfare Information Center
Vegan Action
Vegetarian Pages
Vegetarian Resource Center
Vegetarian Resource Group
VETAIR Foundation
Veterinary Association for Arbitration and Jurisprudence
Veterinary Cancer Society
Veterinary Circle for 10 (Central Luzon State University)
Veterinary Educational Team Sled Dog Racing
Veterinary Emergency Critical Care Society
Veterinary History Society
Veterinary Information Network
Veterinary Medical Association of New York City, Inc.
Veterinary Medical College Application Service
Veterinary Medical Libraries Section - Medical Library
Association
Veterinary Science Club (Cal-Poly)
Veterinary Technician Anesthetist Society
Virginia Tech Pre-Vet Club
Virginia Veterinary Medical Association
Viva Vegetarians International Voice for Animals
Volunteers for Animal Welfare, Inc. (Oklahoma City, OK)
Washington D.C. Humane Society
Washington Ornithological Society
Washington Protection Association
Washington State Veterinary Medical Association
West Point Veterinary Medical Society
West Suburban Humane Society (Chicago, IL)
West Virginia Raptor Rehabilitation Center
Western Canadian Veterinary Students' Association
Whidbey Animals' Improvement Foundation (Washington)
Whiskers Animal Benevolent League (NY)
Wild About Cats
Wilding Heritage Farm
Wildlife Conservation Society (Bronx Zoo)
Wildlife Disease Association
Wildlife Preservation Trust International
Wildlife Support Group (Mississippi State University CVM)
Wildlife Waystation
Winn Feline Foundation
Winnipeg Humane Society
Wisconsin Chow Chow Rescue
Wisconsin Humane Society
World Animal Net Directory
World Aquaculture Society

154

World Association for Buiatrics
World Association of Veterinary Educators
World Federation of Parasitologists
World Small Animal Veterinary Association World Society for the
Protection of Animals
World Veterinary Association
World Wildlife Fund
World Wildlife Fund - Canada
WWW Virtual Library: Animal health, well-being, and rights
WWW Virtual Library: Biology Societies and Organizations

Printed in the United States
80288LV00005B/4

9 781430 315858